Early praise for *Concurrent Data Processing in Elixir*

Concurrent Data Processing in Elixir is the perfect in-depth guide and a comprehensive approach on dealing with data in Elixir, covering both simple and complex scenarios at scale. It's definitely the new companion guide for anyone looking into building modern data pipelines.

➤ **Marcelo Lebre**
   CTO, Remote

An excellent guide to data processing in Elixir. Svilen's writing is engaging and to the point. I would recommend this to both beginner and experienced Elixir programmers alike.

➤ **Sean Moriarity**
   SM Computing LLC

This book is a great place to go beyond the basics and further explore what is arguably the most important aspect of Elixir.

➤ **Saša Jurić**
   Author of *Elixir in Action*

This book was a great read. It certainly delivers what it promises. If you have basic knowledge on OTP and want to improve your concurrency skills, this book is for you!

➤ **Marlus Saraiva**
   Software Engineer, Dashbit

Processes and concurrency are at the heart of the Elixir programming language. Svilen Gospodinov has done a brilliant job at summarizing in a clean and simple way an otherwise complex topic. *Concurrent Data Processing in Elixir* is a must-read for every developer who wants to learn about building high-performant applications within the Elixir ecosystem.

➤ **Velina Petrova**
   Web Developer, Mindvalley

The concurrency model in Elixir is the feature that keeps driving developers and the industry to adopting this fantastic language. *Concurrent Data Processing in Elixir* brings that model to an accessible and practical level by shedding light on harder-to-grasp concepts like supervision tree design and process communication. *Concurrent Data Processing in Elixir* is a must-have for any Elixir developer wanting to gain the performance and reliability of the BEAM.

➤ **Amos King**
   CEO, BinaryNoggin

Concurrent Data Processing in Elixir

Fast, Resilient Applications with OTP,
GenState, Flow, and Broadway

Svilen Gospodinov

The Pragmatic Bookshelf

Raleigh, North Carolina

Many of the designations used by manufacturers and sellers to distinguish their products are claimed as trademarks. Where those designations appear in this book, and The Pragmatic Programmers, LLC was aware of a trademark claim, the designations have been printed in initial capital letters or in all capitals. The Pragmatic Starter Kit, The Pragmatic Programmer, Pragmatic Programming, Pragmatic Bookshelf, PragProg and the linking *g* device are trademarks of The Pragmatic Programmers, LLC.

Every precaution was taken in the preparation of this book. However, the publisher assumes no responsibility for errors or omissions, or for damages that may result from the use of information (including program listings) contained herein.

For our complete catalog of hands-on, practical, and Pragmatic content for software developers, please visit *https://pragprog.com*.

The team that produced this book includes:

CEO: Dave Rankin
COO: Janet Furlow
Managing Editor: Tammy Coron
Series Editor: Bruce A. Tate
Development Editor: Jacquelyn Carter
Copy Editor: Karen Galle
Indexing: Potomac Indexing, LLC
Layout: Gilson Graphics
Founders: Andy Hunt and Dave Thomas

For sales, volume licensing, and support, please contact *support@pragprog.com*.

For international rights, please contact *rights@pragprog.com*.

ISBN-13: 978-1-68050-819-2
Book version: P1.0—August 2021

Contents

Foreword

Elixir started as a learning exercise. I wanted to dive into the Erlang Virtual Machine, and creating a new language would also allow me to explore how programming languages actually work. It was a period where multiple mistakes were made but they were essential in discovering what Elixir should be.

Once the general vision of the language was established, I got the approval to start working on it part time. I personally had the ambition of using it for building scalable and robust web applications. However, I didn't want Elixir to be tied to the web. My goal was to design a general purpose and extensible programming language, allowing developers to bring it to new domains and create a diverse ecosystem.

The Erlang platform has been used extensively for networking and distributed systems since its inception. This meant Elixir would naturally be a good fit in those domains, and building data-processing and data-ingestion pipelines were a natural extension of those areas. In fact, projects like Riak[1] and Disco[2] have already explored using the Erlang platform for working with data at large scales, although they were always presented as complete solutions, and I wanted Elixir to focus on providing a bottom-up approach.

After Elixir v1.0 was released, the Elixir team and I finally started turning our attention to this problem. At the same time, projects like Reactive Extensions[3] from Microsoft and Reactive Streams[4] in the JVM were already brewing important discussions on abstractions for asynchronous data streams with back-pressure. After exploring a couple solutions we finally landed on Gen-Stage,[5] a new behaviour—built on top of GenServer—for exchanging events with back-pressure between Elixir processes.

---

1.   https://riak.com/
2.   https://discoproject.org/
3.   https://en.wikipedia.org/wiki/ReactiveX
4.   https://www.reactive-streams.org/
5.   https://elixir-lang.org/blog/2016/07/14/announcing-genstage/

To provide a more practical example of how GenStage could be used at scale, we also built Flow,[6] a high-level abstraction where you express how to work on collections of data concurrently using known idioms such as map, reduce, and friends, which is automatically converted to a GenStage topology. Flow took its inspiration from projects such as Apache Spark[7] and Apache Beam.[8]

Our initial foray into the data domain has been a success. Companies such as Discord[9] and change.org[10] have stated those libraries play a crucial role in their architecture and in their adoption of the language. This exploration also led to direct improvements to Elixir, namely the Registry and Task.async_stream/2 included in Elixir v1.4.[11]

However, there was still one missing piece.

While GenStage provided developers the building blocks for large abstractions, and Flow gave developers the flexibility to build complex data aggregation pipelines, we were still missing a library that provided a clear and predefined data pipeline, where all you have to do is add the missing pieces instead of assembling it all by yourself. To fill this gap, the Dashbit team built Broadway,[12] with direct feedback from our clients who have been developing and running large data pipelines at scale.

As you can see, a lot of work has been done since GenStage was announced in 2016, and I believe this book is the missing piece to our data ecosystem. It provides developers a focused and unified guide on all the different options to tackle data in Elixir.

Data is never a solved problem, and we welcome you to be part of our journey as you read this.

José Valim (representing both Elixir and Dashbit teams)
Chief Adoption Officer at Dashbit, Creator of Elixir

Tenczynek, Poland, April 2021

---

6. https://github.com/dashbitco/flow/
7. https://spark.apache.org/
8. https://beam.incubator.apache.org/
9. https://elixir-lang.org/blog/2020/10/08/real-time-communication-at-scale-with-elixir-at-discord/
10. https://elixir-lang.org/blog/2020/10/27/delivering-social-change-with-elixir-at-change.org/
11. https://elixir-lang.org/blog/2017/01/05/elixir-v1-4-0-released/
12. https://github.com/dashbitco/broadway

Acknowledgments

Writing this book has been truly an amazing journey. It is also a journey that I would never have been able to complete without the help of all the people who were involved and supported me along the way.

First of all, I would like to thank everyone in the Erlang and Elixir community who are building and contributing to the language and projects used in this book. Without your work, this book simply wouldn't exist.

I would like to particularly thank José Valim for creating Elixir and for continuously supporting the amazing Elixir community. Thank you also for your technical feedback, advice, and support for this book.

Having Pragmatic Bookshelf as my publisher is a dream come true. I'd like to thank everyone at Pragmatic for making this book a reality. Thank you to Dave Rankin for guiding me through the book proposal process. Huge thanks to Bruce A. Tate, whose feedback at various points was invaluable and helped me expand the focus of the book.

I was lucky to have Jacquelyn Carter as my development editor. Thank you Jackie for making every aspect of this book so much better. I cannot express how much I've learnt from you since we started working together. I can now finally switch my spellchecker to British English.

I'm sincerely grateful to everyone who participated in the technical review for the book, provided technical feedback, caught mistakes early on, and sent me their suggestions to improve the content. Thank you Amos King, Andy Jones, David Pollak, Kim Shrier, Marlus Saraiva, Tom Conroy, Tony Daly, Sean Moriarity, and Velina Petrova.

To everyone who bought the Beta version of the book and reached out to me in various ways with corrections, suggestions, or just to tell me how much they enjoyed reading it—thank you so much, your messages mean a lot to me, and helped make this book better.

I'm especially grateful to Marcelo Lebre and Saša Jurić who helped me out on a very short notice. Thank you Marcelo and Saša.

Thank you Dimitar Stanimiroff. Our work on Heresy laid the foundation for this book and is the reason why I decided to write a book in the first place. But above all, thank you for your support and help when I needed it.

Finally, I would like to thank my wife, Emiko. This book is dedicated to you. Thank you always for your kindness, inspiration, love, and support. I'm lucky to have you in my life.

Introduction

Data processing is an essential part of many software applications. In fact, most engineers don't even think about it as something separate from programming. But if you're transforming information in some way, for example, when doing reporting, data aggregation, or analytics, then you're doing data processing.

Thanks to the Erlang Virtual Machine (also known as the BEAM), everyone who uses Elixir benefits from its amazing concurrency model, which is particularly well suited for long-running, concurrent tasks. As a result, you will find that Elixir offers more ways for performing concurrent work than other languages.

While this is a good thing, it could also be challenging to find the right tool for the job. Some tasks are excellent fit for Flow, while others are perfect for Broadway. Sometimes it's easier to just use GenStage, or even the Task module. Making the right choice means going through dozens of pages of documentation, and that would be just the beginning.

This book is here to help you navigate the world of concurrency tools available in the Elixir ecosystem. You will learn about the most popular modules and libraries and start using them in no time. You will also discover a range of new techniques that will help you simplify your product, improve the performance of your code, and make your application more resilient to errors and increased workloads.

Who Should Read This Book?

Most applications have to process data in some way and run on machines with multi-core CPUs. If your application is one of them, and data processing plays an important part in what you do, then this book is for you. Web development is very popular with Elixir, but the techniques in this book work equally well if you're using Nerves and working on embedded software.

This book is targeted at intermediate developers, who are comfortable with writing Elixir code. If you're not familiar with the language, then you should pick another book, such as *Programming Elixir 1.6 [Tho18]* by Dave Thomas, before attempting this one.

However, you don't have to be an expert in Elixir—this book will guide you through each topic with plenty of examples and helpful figures along the way. In every chapter, you will gain valuable knowledge which you can then apply to your personal or business projects.

About This Book

There are five chapters, each dedicated to a specific module or a library.

In Chapter 1, Easy Concurrency with the Task Module, on page 1, you'll get started on the journey of learning how concurrency works in Elixir. It introduces the Task module, processes, timeouts, and other topics that lay the foundation for the following chapters to build upon.

In Chapter 2, Long-Running Processes Using GenServer, on page 25 you'll learn about GenServer and supervisors. You will see how to create and configure GenServer processes by building a simple job-processing system. We'll introduce the Supervisor behaviour and talk about how Elixir achieves fault tolerance.

In Chapter 3, Data-Processing Pipelines with GenStage, on page 57 we'll move on to data-processing pipelines. You will learn about back-pressure, and the building blocks of GenStage—producer, consumer, and producer-consumer. You will also start building your very own web scraper by putting what you have learned into practice.

In Chapter 4, Processing Collections with Flow, on page 89, you'll see how you can use Flow instead of GenStage for operations like map, filter, reduce, and more. You will learn how to use it when working with large datasets and even plug it into existing GenStage data-processing pipelines.

The last chapter is Chapter 5, Data-Ingestion Pipelines with Broadway, on page 113. We're going to set up a data-ingestion pipeline using RabbitMQ, but the techniques apply to other message brokers, such as Amazon SQS, Apache Kafka, and Google Cloud Pub/Sub. We will cover the various options and benefits that come with Broadway.

About the Code

You can't apply all the techniques in this book without having data to process or services to integrate with. At the same time, downloading large data sets or signing up to third-party services is too cumbersome and not practical for the purposes of this book. That's why all projects attempt to simulate real-world cases, so you can focus on the implementation details. It also makes them easy to reproduce.

To run the code examples and snippets from the book on your computer, make sure you have Erlang and Elixir installed first. The versions used in this book are Erlang 23.0 and Elixir 1.11. If you need help installing them, check Elixir's official website[1] to see what installation options you have for your operating system.

For Chapter 5, you will also need RabbitMQ installed. You can find installation instructions on RabbitMQ's website.[2]

Online Resources

All examples and source code can be downloaded from the book page on the Pragmatic Bookshelf website.[3] Please report any errors or suggestions you may have using the errata link.[4]

If you enjoyed reading this book, please let others know about it and spread the word. If you use Twitter, you can find me at @svileng[5] and let me know which part of the book you liked the most. You can also tweet to @pragprog.[6]

Svilen Gospodinov
London, United Kingdom, August 2021

---

1. https://elixir-lang.org/install.html
2. https://www.rabbitmq.com/download.html
3. https://pragprog.com/book/sgdpelixir
4. https://pragprog.com/book/sgdpelixir/errata
5. https://twitter.com/svileng
6. https://twitter.com/pragprog

CHAPTER 1

Easy Concurrency with the Task Module

Since the dawn of the computer industry, hardware manufacturers and computer scientists have tried to make computers faster at running programs. At first, multithreading was the only way to achieve concurrency, which is the ability to run two or more programming tasks and switch between them to collect the results. This is how computers appeared to be doing many things at once, when in fact they were simply multitasking.

Multi-core CPUs changed that. They brought parallelism and allowed tasks to run at the same time, independently, which significantly increased systems' performance. Multiprocessor architectures followed, enabling even greater concurrency and parallelism by supporting two or more CPUs on a single machine. The figure below shows a simple comparison between concurrency on a single-core CPU vs. a dual-core CPU. The latter also enables parallelism:

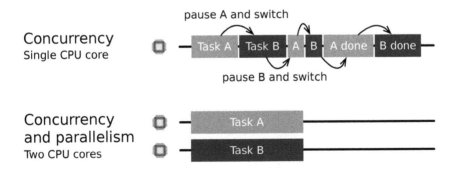

Of course, cutting-edge hardware always comes with a high price tag. But with the advent of cloud computing, things changed once again. Nowadays you can run code on cloud services using virtual machines with dozens of CPU cores, without the need to buy and maintain any physical hardware.

All these advancements are important to us as software engineers. We want to write software that performs well and runs quickly. After all, no one likes loading screens and waiting for the computer to finish. However, running code on a multi-core processor system does not automatically make it efficient. In order to take full advantage of the computer resources available to us, we need to write software with concurrency and parallelism in mind. Thankfully, modern programming languages try to help us as much as possible, and Elixir is no exception. In fact, thanks to Erlang, the Erlang Virtual Machine (BEAM), and the Open Telecom Platform (OTP), Elixir is a superb choice for building concurrent applications and processing data as you'll soon see in this and upcoming chapters.

In this book we're going to cover the most popular tools for performing concurrent work using Elixir. You will learn about the pros and cons of each one and see how they work in practice. Some of them, like the Task module and GenServer, come with Elixir. The others—GenStage, Flow, and Broadway—are available as stand-alone libraries on the Hex.pm package registry. Knowing how to utilize each of these tools will help you leverage concurrency in the most effective way and solve even the most challenging problems. Along the way, you will also learn how to build fault-tolerant applications, recover from failures, use back-pressure to deal with limited system resources, and many more useful techniques.

First, we are going to look at the Task module, which is part of the Elixir standard library. It has a powerful set of features that will help you run code concurrently. You are also going to see how to handle errors and prevent the application from crashing when a concurrent task crashes. The chapter provides a foundation on which the following chapters will be built upon, so let's get started!

Introducing the Task Module

To run code concurrently in Elixir, you have to start a process and execute your code within that process. You may also need to retrieve the result and use it for something else. Elixir provides a low-level function and a macro for doing this—spawn/1 and receive. However, using them could be tricky in practice, and you will likely end up with a lot of repetitive code.

Elixir also ships with a module called Task, which significantly simplifies starting concurrent processes. It provides an abstraction for running code concurrently, retrieving results, handling errors and starting a series of processes. It packs a lot of features and has a concise API, so there is rarely (if ever) need to use the more primitive spawn/1 and receive.

In this chapter, we are going to cover everything that the Task module has to offer. You will learn how to start tasks, and different ways to retrieve results. You will tackle processing large lists of data. We will talk about handling failure and explain how process linking works in Elixir. You will then see how to use one of the built-in Supervisor modules for isolating process crashes, and finally, discuss Elixir's approach to error handling.

Before we dive in, let's create an Elixir project to work on first and get familiar with some of the development tools we're going to use throughout this and the following chapters.

What Is an Elixir Process?

 Processes in Elixir are Erlang processes, since Elixir runs on the Erlang Virtual Machine. Unlike operating system processes, they are very lightweight in terms of memory usage and quick to start. The Erlang VM knows how to run them concurrently and in parallel (when a multi-core CPU is present). As a result, by using processes, you get concurrency and parallelism for free.

Creating Our Playground

We are going to create an application called sender and pretend that we are sending emails to real email addresses. We are going to use the Task module later to develop some of its functionality.

First, let's use the mix command-line tool to scaffold our new project:

```
$ mix new sender --sup
```

This creates a sender directory with a bunch of files and folders inside. Notice that we also used the --sup argument, which will create an application with a *supervision tree*. You will learn about supervision trees later in this chapter.

Next, change your current directory to sender with cd sender and run iex -S mix. You should see some Erlang version information and the following message:

```
Interactive Elixir (1.11.0) - press Ctrl+C to exit (type h() ENTER for help)
iex(1)>
```

We're now running the *Interactive Elixir* shell, also known as IEx. We are going to use it to test code frequently throughout the book. Most of the time, when we make a code change using our text editor, we can call the special recompile/0 function available in IEx, and the code will reload:

```
iex(1)> recompile()
:noop
```

We haven't actually added or changed any code yet, so the function returned just :noop for *no operation.*

In some cases, you may need to restart the IEx shell entirely, for example, when making fundamental application changes in the application.ex file. You can restart IEx by pressing Ctrl-C twice to quit and then running the iex -S mix command again.

To keep our project and examples simple, we're not actually going to send real emails. However, we still need some business logic for our experiments. We can use the Process.sleep/1 function to pretend we're sending an email, which is normally a slow operation and can take a few seconds to complete. When called with an integer, Process.sleep/1 stops the current process for the given amount of time in milliseconds. This is very handy, because you can use it to simulate code that takes a long time to complete. You can also use it to test various edge cases, as you will see later. Of course, in real world production applications, you will replace this with your actual business logic. But for now, let's pretend that we're doing some very intensive work.

Let's open sender.ex and add the following:

```
sender/lib/sender.ex
def send_email(email) do
  Process.sleep(3000)
  IO.puts("Email to #{email} sent")
  {:ok, "email_sent"}
end
```

Calling this function will pause execution for three seconds and print a message, which will be useful to debugging. It also returns a tuple {:ok, "email_sent"} to indicate that the email was successfully sent.

Now that everything is set up, we're ready to start. I suggest you keep one terminal session with IEx open and your favorite text editor next to it, so you can make and run changes as we go.

Starting Tasks and Retrieving Results

Before jumping into the Task module, let's see how things work at the moment. Let's call the send_email/1 function from IEx, and pass a fictional email address as an argument. Don't forget to run the recompile() command first if you've been running IEx already:

```
iex> recompile()
Compiling 1 file (.ex)
:ok
```

```
iex> Sender.send_email("hello@world.com")
Email to hello@world.com sent
{:ok, "email_sent"}
```

Did you notice the delay? We had to wait three seconds until we saw the printed output and result. In fact, even the iex> prompt was not showing. Let's add another function, notify_all/1:

```
sender/lib/sender.ex
def notify_all(emails) do
  Enum.each(emails, &send_email/1)
end
```

The notify_all/1 function uses Enum.each/2 to iterate over the variable emails, which is a list of strings. For each item in the list, we are going to call the send_email/1 function. We are going to test this function in IEx, but first we need some test data. Create a file .iex.exs in the main project folder sender at the top level where mix.exs is also located. Add the following:

```
sender/.iex.exs
emails = [
  "hello@world.com",
  "hola@world.com",
  "nihao@world.com",
  "konnichiwa@world.com",
]
```

Once you save the file, quit IEx and start it again with iex -S mix. Type emails and press enter to inspect the variable:

```
iex(1)> emails
["hello@world.com", "hola@world.com", "nihao@world.com",
 "konnichiwa@world.com"]
```

This will save you a lot of typing. All Elixir code in .iex.exs will run when IEx starts, so this will persist between IEx sessions. Now let's use the test data with notify_all/1. Can you guess how much time it will take to send all emails? Let's find out:

```
iex> Sender.notify_all(emails)
Email to hello@world.com sent
Email to hola@world.com sent
Email to nihao@world.com sent
Email to konnichiwa@world.com sent
:ok
```

It took four calls to send_email/1 and about twelve seconds to complete. Just waiting for the output in IEx felt like ages. This is not good at all. As our user base grows, it will take forever to send our emails.

Don't despair—we can significantly speed up our code using the Task module. However, before we jump into it, let's take a moment to talk about two important concepts in programming: *synchronous* and *asynchronous* code.

Synchronous and Asynchronous Code

By default, when you run some code in Elixir, you have to wait for it to complete. You cannot do anything in the meantime, and you get the result as soon as code has finished. The code is executed *synchronously* and is sometimes called *blocking code*.

The opposite of this is running code *asynchronously*. In this case, you ask the programming runtime to run the code, but carry on with the rest of the program. Asynchronous code runs in the *background* because the application keeps running, as if nothing happened. Eventually, when the asynchronous code finishes, you can retrieve the result. Because asynchronous code does not block the main execution of the program, it is called *non-blocking code*. Asynchronous code is also concurrent, since it enables us to continue doing other work. The figure below illustrates the difference between synchronous and asynchronous code in a bread-making program:

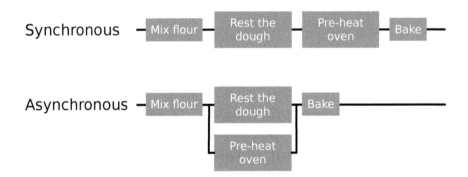

Since only the final step Bake requires the oven to be preheated, you can run Pre-heat oven asynchronously and do something else in the meantime. Compared to the synchronous version, this significantly decreases the time needed to complete the set of instructions.

You may have guessed already that the notify_all/1 function is sending each email synchronously. This is why it is taking so long to complete. To improve this, we're going to convert our code to run asynchronously. Thanks to Elixir's Task module, we will need only a few small changes to achieve that. Let's see how it works.

Starting Processes

The Task module contains a number of very useful functions for running code asynchronously and concurrently. One of them is start/1. It accepts a function as an argument, and inside that function we should do all the work we intend to do. Let's try it out quickly in IEx:

```
iex> Task.start(fn -> IO.puts("Hello async world!") end)
Hello async world!
{:ok, #PID<0.266.0>}
```

You saw the message printed instantly because it's a quick operation, but the actual result was {:ok, #PID<0.266.0>}. Returning a tuple like {:ok, result} or {:error, message} is a common practice in Elixir. The result was :ok for success and #PID<0.266.0>. *PID* stands for *process identifier*—a number that uniquely identifies an Elixir process.

We already have send_email/1 ready, so we can use Task.start/1 to call it. Let's make some changes:

sender/lib/sender.change1.ex
```
def notify_all(emails) do
  Enum.each(emails, fn email ->
    Task.start(fn ->
      send_email(email)
    end)
  end)
end
```

Then recompile and run notify_all/1:

```
iex> Sender.notify_all(emails)
:ok
Email to hello@world.com sent
Email to hola@world.com sent
Email to nihao@world.com sent
Email to konnichiwa@world.com sent
```

This should be significantly faster—in fact, four times faster! All functions were called concurrently and finished at the same time, printing the success message as we expected.

Retrieving the Result of a Task

Task.start/1 has one limitation by design: it does not return the result of the function that was executed. This may be useful in some cases, but most of the time you need the result for something else. It would be great if we modify our code and return a meaningful result when all emails are sent successfully.

To retrieve the result of a function, you have to use Task.async/1. It returns a %Task{} struct which you can assign to a variable for later use. You can give it a try in IEx like so:

```
iex> task = Task.async(fn -> Sender.send_email("hello@world.com") end)
%Task{
  owner: #PID<0.145.0>,
  pid: #PID<0.165.0>,
  ref: #Reference<0.713486762.1657274369.63141>
}
```

The send_email/1 code is now running in the background. In the meantime, we are free to do other work as needed. You can add more business logic or even start other tasks. When you need the actual result of the task, you can retrieve it using the task variable. Let's have a closer look at what this variable contains:

- owner is the PID of the process that started the Task process.
- pid is the identifier of the Task process itself.
- ref is the *process monitor reference.*

Process monitoring is out of the scope of this book. However, it is worth knowing that you can monitor a process and receive notifications from it using a reference value—for example, when and how a process exits.

To retrieve the result of the task, you can use either Task.await/1 or Task.yield/1 which accept a Task struct as an argument. There is an important difference in the way await/1 and yield/1 work, so you have to choose wisely. They both stop the program and try to retrieve the result of the task. The difference comes from the way they handle *process timeouts.*

Process timeouts ensure that processes don't get stuck waiting forever. To show how they work, let's increase the time the send_email/1 function takes to 30 seconds, just temporarily:

```
def send_email(email) do
  Process.sleep(30_000)
  IO.puts("Email to #{email} sent")
  {:ok, "email_sent"}
end
```

Then recompile/0 in IEx. We're now going to run the code asynchronously and pipe the task result into await/1:

```
iex> Task.async(fn -> Sender.send_email("hi@world.com") end) |> Task.await()
```

After five seconds, you will receive an exception similar to this one:

```
** (exit) exited in: Task.await(%Task{owner: #PID<0.144.0>,
  pid: #PID<0.151.0>,
```

```
ref: #Reference<0.2297312895.3696492546.156249>}, 5000)
  ** (EXIT) time out
  (elixir) lib/task.ex:607: Task.await/2
```

When using await/1 we expect a task to finish within a certain amount of time. By default, this time is set to 5000ms, which is five seconds. You can change that by passing an integer with the amount of milliseconds as a second argument, for example Task.await(task, 10_000). You can also disable the timeout by passing the atom :infinity.

In comparison, Task.yield/1 simply returns nil if the task hasn't completed. The timeout of yield/1 is also 5000ms but does not cause an exception and crash. You can also do Task.yield(task) repeatedly to check for a result, which is not allowed by await/1. A completed task will return either {:ok, result} or {:exit, reason}. You can see this in action:

```
iex> task = Task.async(fn -> Sender.send_email("hi@world.com") end)
%Task{
  owner: #PID<0.135.0>,
  pid: #PID<0.147.0>,
  ref: #Reference<0.3033103973.1551368196.24818>
}
iex> Task.yield(task)
nil
iex> Task.yield(task)
nil

Email to hi@world.com sent
iex> Task.yield(task)
{:ok, {:ok, "email_sent"}}
iex> Task.yield(task)
nil
```

This output illustrates what happens when you call Task.yield/1 while the task is still running—you receive nil. Once the success message is printed out, we received {:ok, {:ok, "email_sent"}} as expected. You can also use yield/2 and provide your own timeout, similarly to await/2, but the :infinity option is not allowed. Note that you only get the result from yield/1 once, and subsequent calls will return nil.

You may be wondering what happens if our task is stuck and never finishes? While await/1 takes care of stopping the task, yield/1 will leave it running. It is a good idea to stop the task manually by calling Task.shutdown(task). The shutdown/1 function also accepts a timeout and gives the process a last chance to complete, before stopping it. If it completes, you will receive the result as normal.

You can also stop a process immediately (and rather violently) by using the atom :brutal_kill as a second argument.

As you can see, using yield/1 and shutdown/1 is a bit more work than await/1. Which one to use depends on your use case. Very often a task timeout justifies an exception, in which case await/1 will be more convenient to use. Whenever you require more control over the timeout and shutdown, you can switch to yield/1 and shutdown/1. The important part is that after using async/1, you should always process the result, using either await/1, or yield/1 followed by shutdown/1.

For our notify_all/1 logic, we're going to use await/1 for simplicity. Remember to revert our previous change in send_email/1 and set Process.sleep/1 back to 3000ms:

```
def send_email(email) do
  Process.sleep(3000)
```

Now we're going to replace Task.start/1 with Task.async/1:

```
sender/lib/sender.change2.ex
def notify_all(emails) do
  emails
  |> Enum.map(fn email ->
    Task.async(fn ->
      send_email(email)
    end)
  end)
  |> Enum.map(&Task.await/1)
end
```

Notice that we're also using Enum.map/2 instead of Enum.each/2, because we want to map each email string to its corresponding Task struct. The struct is needed to retrieve the result from each process.

We used the Elixir shorthand function syntax here—&Task.await/1. If you are not familiar with it, it is simply equivalent to writing:

```
Enum.map(fn task ->
  Task.await(task)
end)
```

Let's try out the latest changes in IEx:

```
iex> Sender.notify_all(emails)
Email to hello@world.com sent
Email to hola@world.com sent
Email to nihao@world.com sent
Email to konnichiwa@world.com sent
[ok: "email_sent", ok: "email_sent", ok: "email_sent", ok: "email_sent"]
```

The function returned a list of results. For each task you have an ok: "email_sent" tuple, which is what the send_email/1 function returns. In your business logic, you can return an {:error, "error message"} when something goes wrong. Then you will be able to collect the error and potentially retry the operation or do something else with the result.

Creating tasks from lists of items is actually very common in Elixir. In the next section, we are going to use a function specifically designed for doing this. It also offers a range of additional features, especially useful when working with large lists. Keep reading.

Keyword Lists in Elixir

 Elixir has a special notation for lists containing key-value tuples, also known as keyword lists.[1] Each item in the keyword list must be a two-element tuple. The first element is the key name, which must be an atom. The second is the value and can be of any type. They are displayed in IEx without the curly braces, like this [ok: "email_sent"]. This is equivalent to [{:ok, "email_sent"}].

Managing Series of Tasks

Let's imagine we have one million users and we want to send an email to all of them. We can use Enum.map/2 and Task.async/1 like we did before, but starting one million processes will put sudden pressure on our system resources. It can degrade the system's performance and potentially make other services unresponsive. Our email service provider will not be happy either, because we also put a lot of pressure on their email infrastructure.

On the other hand, we don't want to send emails one by one, because it is slow and inefficient. It seems that we are at a crossroad, and whichever way we take, we end up in peril. We don't want to choose between performance and reliability—we want to be able to run Task processes to leverage concurrency, but ensure we do not overload our system resources as we scale our product and increase our user base.

The solution to our problems is async_stream/3. It's another very handy function from the Task module which is designed to create task processes from a list of items. For every item in the list, async_stream/3 will start a process and run the function we provide to process the item. It works just like Enum.map/2 and Task.async/2 combined, with one major difference: you can set a limit on the

---

1. https://elixir-lang.org/getting-started/keywords-and-maps.html

number of processes running at the same time. The figure below illustrates how this works:

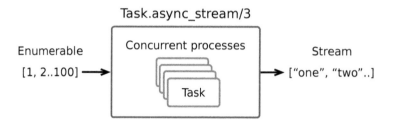

In this example, the concurrency limit is set to four, so even if you have a list of one hundred items, at most only four processes will run concurrently at any given time. This is an example of handling *back-pressure*, which we are going to discuss in-depth in Chapter 3, Data-Processing Pipelines with Gen-Stage, on page 57. For now, all you need to know is this strategy of handling processes is great at preventing sudden spikes of system usage. In other words, you get concurrency and performance without sacrificing reliability.

As the function name suggests, async_stream/3 returns a Stream. Streams in Elixir are data structures that hold one or more operations that don't run immediately, only when explicitly told so. That's why they're sometimes called *lazy enumerables*. Let's see what happens when we run this function from IEx:

```
iex> Task.async_stream(emails, &Sender.send_email/1)
#Function<1.35903181/2 in Task.build_stream/3>
```

Instead of the usual result, we received a function, which is going to create a Stream. It's important to understand how streams work, so let's run another quick example in IEx:

```
iex> Stream.map([1, 2, 3], & &1 * 2)
#Stream<[
  enum: [1, 2, 3],
  funs: [#Function<49.33009823/1 in Stream.map/2>]
]>
```

If we have used Enum.map/2 the function would have returned [2, 4, 6]. Instead, the result stream simply contains the initial input and a list of operations funs. These operations can be run at a later time. Because both Stream and Enum implement the Enumerable protocol, many Enum functions have a lazy alternative in the Stream module.

One way to run a stream is to use the Stream.run/1 function. However, Stream.run/1 always returns :ok so it is only useful when you are not interested in the final result. Instead, you can use Enum.to_list/1, which will try to convert the stream to a List data structure. As a result of this conversion, all operations in the stream will run, and the result will be returned as a list. Other functions in the Enum module will also force the stream to run, such as Enum.reduce/3. You can use them if you intend to do more work with the result.

Why Does async_stream Return a Stream?

Streams are designed to emit a series of values, one by one. As soon as Task.async_stream/3 finds out that a task process has completed, it will emit the result and take the next element from the input, starting a new process. This means it can maintain a number of concurrent events, which is one of the benefits of async_stream/3. You can also use all other functions from the Stream module to compose complex data-processing flows.

Now, let's update notify_all/1 to use async_stream/3. This time, however, we will run the stream using Enum.to_list/1:

```
sender/lib/sender.change3.ex
def notify_all(emails) do
  emails
  |> Task.async_stream(&send_email/1)
  |> Enum.to_list()
end
```

And give it a go in IEx, but don't forget to recompile/0 first:

```
iex> Sender.notify_all(emails)
Email to hello@world.com sent
Email to hola@world.com sent
Email to nihao@world.com sent
Email to konnichiwa@world.com sent
[
  ok: {:ok, "email_sent"},
  ok: {:ok, "email_sent"},
  ok: {:ok, "email_sent"},
  ok: {:ok, "email_sent"}
]
```

As you can see, the output is similar to the one from the Task.async/2 example. However, depending on how many logical cores your machine has, the time it takes for the function to complete may be different.

As we mentioned before, async_stream/3 maintains a limit on how many processes can be running at the same time. By default, this limit is set to the number of logical cores available in the system. Previously we used Task.async/2 to manually start a process for each of the four items. This means that if you have a CPU with less than four logical cores, async_stream/3 will appear to be slower. You can easily change this default behavior through the optional max_concurrency parameter. Let's set max_concurrency to 1 temporarily:

```
|> Task.async_stream(&send_email/1, max_concurrency: 1)
```

When you try the new changes again, you will see that emails are sent out one by one. This is not very useful in practice, but it demonstrates how max_concurrency works. You can revert the change or set it to an even higher number. In production applications, you can benchmark if higher max_concurrency works better for your use case, taking into consideration your system resources and need for performance.

Another option that needs mentioning is :ordered. Currently, async_stream/3 assumes we want the results in the same order as they were originally. This order preservation can potentially slow down our processing, because async_stream/3 will wait for a slow process to complete before moving on to the next.

In our case, we only need the results to check if an email was successfully sent or not. We don't necessarily need them in exactly the same order. We can potentially speed things up by disabling ordering like so:

```
|> Task.async_stream(&send_email/1, ordered: false)
```

Now async_stream/3 won't be idle if one process is taking longer than others.

Processes started by async_stream/3 are also subject to timeouts, just like those started by start/1 and async/2. The :timeout optional parameter is supported and defaults to 5000ms. When a task reaches the timeout, it will produce an exception, stopping the stream and crashing the current process. This behavior can be changed using an optional :on_timeout argument, which you can set to :kill_task. This argument is similar to the :brutal_kill one supported by Task.shutdown/2. Here is an example:

```
|> Task.async_stream(&send_email/1, on_timeout: :kill_task)
```

As a result of using the :kill_task option, when a process exits with a timeout, async_stream/3 will ignore it and carry on as normal.

A process can crash for many reasons. We talked about timeout exceptions, which happen when the processes take too long to complete. This could be because the work it is doing is very time consuming or because it is waiting for a slow third-party API to respond. Sometimes it is an unexpected error that causes an exception. The important thing is that when a process crashes, it can also crash the process that started it, which in turn crashes its parent process, triggering a chain reaction that can ultimately crash your whole application.

This sounds like a programming disaster waiting to happen, but the good news is that Elixir, thanks to Erlang, has a set of powerful tools to manage processes, catch crashes, and recover quickly. In the next section, we are going to explain why this chain reaction is a good thing, how to isolate it, and how to use it to our advantage. You will also start learning how to build the fault-tolerant applications Elixir is famous for.

Linking Processes

Processes in Elixir can be linked together, and Task processes are usually automatically linked to the process that started them. This link is simply called a *process link*. Process links have an important role when building concurrent and fault-tolerant applications. They help us immediately shut down parts of the system, or even the whole system when needed, preventing the application from running with a bad state. Let's see why process links are useful and how they work by looking at a few examples. The following figure shows three processes linked together:

As you can see, Process C has just crashed. Imagine that Process B continues running, unaware of the crash. It is expecting to receive a result from Process C and report back to Process A. However, this will never happen, so this system is left in a bad state.

This can be avoided thanks to process linking. When two processes are linked, they form a special relationship—as soon as one exits, the other will be notified. When you have a chain of linked processes, all of them will be eventually notified when a crash happens. By default, linked processes will terminate and clean up the memory they use, preventing other potential problems down the line. This means that the crash of Process C will trigger a chain reaction and Process B will terminate, followed by Process A.

However, a chain reaction like this only makes sense when a severe error happens. Take a look at the figure on page 16, which shows running processes for a banking web application.

Most web applications rely heavily on a database, and access to the database is usually managed by a process. In this example, the Repo process has this responsibility. If Repo crashes, because the database becomes unavailable,

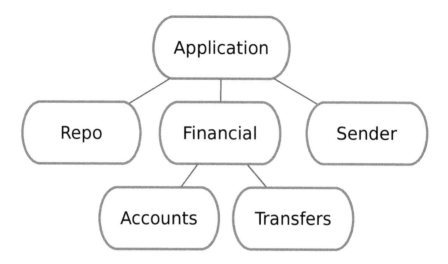

this application won't be able to work at all. If that ever happens, you can let all processes terminate, which will bring the website offline.

Now, let's consider the process Sender, which is responsible for sending emails. Unlike the Repo process, it is not vital in giving users access to their bank account. If the Sender process crashes for whatever reason, we don't want to shut down the whole application. We want to contain this crash and let the rest of the system carry on.

You can isolate crashes by configuring a process to *trap exits*. Trapping an exit means acknowledging the exit message of a linked process, but continuing to run instead of terminating. This also means the exit message will not be propagated further to other processes. Going back to our original example—if Process B is configured to trap exits, it will continue working after the crash of Process C, keeping Process A safe as well. You can configure a process to trap exits manually, but usually you want to use a special type of process called a *supervisor*. We are going to talk about supervisors in just a moment.

As you can see, process links are an essential mechanism for detecting exits and dealing with unexpected process crashes. Most utility functions in the Task module create process links automatically, linking to the current process, but there are some that don't. You have the choice to link or not to link to the current process, but you have to choose the right function.

For example, when we used async/1 and async_stream/3, a process link was created for each new process. Task.start/1, on the other hand, does not create a process link, but there is Task.start_link/1 that does just that.

Most functions in the Task module that link to the current process by default have an alternative, usually ending with _nolink. Task.Supervisor.async_nolink/3 is the alternative to Task.async/1. Task.async_stream/3 can be replaced with Task.Supervisor.async_stream_nolink/4. All functions in the Task.Supervisor module are designed to be linked to a supervisor.

Next, we're going to learn about supervisors and how we can use one when starting task processes.

Meeting the Supervisor

Just like in the workplace, where supervisors are held responsible for groups of employees, Elixir supervisors are responsible for the processes assigned to them. Subordinate processes are also required to report back to their supervisor, who has to ensure everything is running smoothly. To accomplish this, supervisors come with a set of features that allow them to effectively manage other processes. They can start and stop processes and restart them in case of unforeseen errors in the system. They are configured to trap exits, so when a supervised process exits with an error, that error will be isolated and it won't propagate further. All this makes supervisors an important building block for fault-tolerant applications.

Supervised processes are called *child processes*. Any OTP process can be supervised and you can also add a supervisor as a child of another supervisor. All you have to do is ask the supervisor to start the process you want to be managed. This allows us to easily build a hierarchy of processes also called a *supervision tree*.

Our sender application already has a supervisor in place, which you can see in application.ex:

```
sender/lib/sender/application.ex
def start(_type, _args) do
  children = [
    # Starts a worker by calling: Sender.Worker.start_link(arg)
    # {Sender.Worker, arg}
  ]

  # See https://hexdocs.pm/elixir/Supervisor.html
  # for other strategies and supported options
  opts = [strategy: :one_for_one, name: Sender.Supervisor]
  Supervisor.start_link(children, opts)
end
```

The start/2 function has some boilerplate code and some instructions already in place. At the end of the function we have Supervisor.start_link(children, opts) that starts the main supervisor of the application. Since the children variable is just an empty list, there are actually no child processes to supervise. This setup is the result of us using the --sup argument when calling the mix new command to create our project.

Now that you know how useful supervisors are, let's see how we can use one for our Task processes. We don't want our current process to crash if a single task crashes, so we will isolate potential errors by starting the tasks' processes under a supervisor.

Adding a Supervisor

Elixir provides a *Supervisor behaviour* for creating supervisor processes, which you have to implement yourself. We are going to do that in Chapter 2, Long-Running Processes Using GenServer, on page 25. However, there are also some built-in supervisors which we can use without writing (almost) any code, and one of them is Task.Supervisor. It's made specifically for working with task processes, so it's an excellent choice for us. Open application.ex and update the children list:

```
sender/lib/sender/application.change1.ex
def start(_type, _args) do
  children = [
    {Task.Supervisor, name: Sender.EmailTaskSupervisor}
  ]

  opts = [strategy: :one_for_one, name: Sender.Supervisor]
  Supervisor.start_link(children, opts)
end
```

The element we added is referred to as a *child specification*. There are different types of formats for writing child specifications, but most of the time it is a tuple, containing information about the child process. This information is used by the supervisor to identify, start, and link the process.

Since Task.Supervisor is a built-in module, our child specification is simply the module name, followed by a list of options. We use the :name option to give it a unique name of our choice, which we will use later. Naming a process is known as *name registration*. It is common to append "Supervisor" when naming supervisors, so we called it Sender.EmailTaskSupervisor.

The child specification could be also be a map. We can rewrite the last change and use a map like this:

```
def start(_type, _args) do
  children = [
    %{
      id: Sender.EmailTaskSupervisor,
      start: {
        Task.Supervisor,
        :start_link,
        [[name: Sender.EmailTaskSupervisor]]
      }
    }
  ]
  opts = [strategy: :one_for_one, name: Sender.Supervisor]
  Supervisor.start_link(children, opts)
end
```

Using a map is more verbose, but it allows you to set other configuration options in the map, in addition to the :id and :start values. There is also a helper function Supervisor.child_spec/1[2] which returns a map and lets you override only the keys you need.

We're going to keep the tuple format for now, but we'll use the other formats too, later in the book.

Our supervisor is now ready to use. It is as simple as that and there is no need to create any files or write more code. This simple change allows us to use a whole array of functions found in the Task.Supervisor module, some of which we introduced earlier.

Using Task.Supervisor

Before we switch to using EmailTaskSupervisor, let's see what happens when an error occurs and there is no supervisor in place. We are going to simulate an error by raising an exception when sending one of our fake emails. Edit sender.ex and add the following function clause just before send_email/1:

```
sender/lib/sender.change4.ex
def send_email("konnichiwa@world.com" = email), do:
  raise "Oops, couldn't send email to #{email}!"

def send_email(email) do
  Process.sleep(3000)
  IO.puts("Email to #{email} sent")
  {:ok, "email_sent"}
end
```

---

2. https://hexdocs.pm/elixir/Supervisor.html#child_spec/2

Using pattern matching, we are going to raise an exception only when the email address is konnichiwa@world.com. Let's see the impact of this error in practice. Restart your IEx shell and run the built-in self/0 function:

```
iex(1)> self()
#PID<0.136.0>
```

You get a process identifier for the current process, which is the IEx shell itself. Your number may be different than mine, but that's okay. Take a note of it.

Now, let's run our notify_all/1 function and see what happens:

```
iex(2)> Sender.notify_all(emails)

[error] Task #PID<0.154.0> started from #PID<0.136.0> terminating
** (RuntimeError) Oops, couldn't send email to konnichiwa@world.com!
  (sender) lib/sender.ex:8: Sender.send_email/1
  (elixir) lib/task/supervised.ex:90: Task.Supervised.invoke_mfa/2
  (elixir) lib/task/supervised.ex:35: Task.Supervised.reply/5
  (stdlib) proc_lib.erl:249: :proc_lib.init_p_do_apply/3
Function: &:erlang.apply/2
  Args: [#Function<0.104978293/1 in Sender.notify_all/1>,
  ["konnichiwa@world.com"]]
** (EXIT from #PID<0.136.0>) shell process exited with reason:
  an exception was raised:
  ** (RuntimeError) Oops, couldn't send email to konnichiwa@world.com!
    (sender) lib/sender.ex:8: Sender.send_email/1
    (elixir) lib/task/supervised.ex:90: Task.Supervised.invoke_mfa/2
    (elixir) lib/task/supervised.ex:35: Task.Supervised.reply/5
    (stdlib) proc_lib.erl:249: :proc_lib.init_p_do_apply/3

iex(1)>
```

That's one big error message. In fact, there are two error messages that seem to be almost identical. Remember what we said about process links and how crashes propagate between linked processes? In this case, a task process linked to IEx raises an exception. Because of this link, created by async_stream/3, IEx also crashed with the same exception message. You can verify this by running self() again:

```
iex(1)> self()
#PID<0.155.0>
```

We have a new process identifier which means that a new IEx process was started and the old one has crashed.

We can prevent this by using the new EmailTaskSupervisor. Change notify_all/1 to use Task.Supervisor.async_stream_nolink/4 instead of Task.async_stream/3:

```
sender/lib/sender.change4.ex
def notify_all(emails) do
  Sender.EmailTaskSupervisor
  |> Task.Supervisor.async_stream_nolink(emails, &send_email/1)
  |> Enum.to_list()
end
```

The new code is very similar to the old one. The first argument of async_stream_nolink/4 is a supervisor module for the task processes—that's where you can use Sender.EmailTaskSupervisor. The rest of the arguments are identical to Task.async_stream/3. Let's run recompile() and notify_all/1 again:

```
iex> Sender.notify_all(emails)

[error] Task #PID<0.173.0> started from #PID<0.155.0> terminating
** (RuntimeError) Oops, couldn't send email to konnichiwa@world.com!
    (sender) lib/sender.ex:8: Sender.send_email/1
    (elixir) lib/task/supervised.ex:90: Task.Supervised.invoke_mfa/2
    (elixir) lib/task/supervised.ex:35: Task.Supervised.reply/5
    (stdlib) proc_lib.erl:249: :proc_lib.init_p_do_apply/3
Function: &:erlang.apply/2
    Args: [#Function<0.32410907/1 in Sender.notify_all/1>,
    ["konnichiwa@world.com"]]

[info]  Email to hello@world.com sent
[info]  Email to hola@world.com sent
[info]  Email to nihao@world.com sent
[
  ok: {:ok, "email_sent"},
  ok: {:ok, "email_sent"},
  ok: {:ok, "email_sent"},
  exit: {%RuntimeError{
    message: "Oops, couldn't send email to konnichiwa@world.com!"
  },
  [
    {Sender, :send_email, 1, [file: 'lib/sender.ex', line: 8]},
    {Task.Supervised, :invoke_mfa, 2,
     [file: 'lib/task/supervised.ex', line: 90]},
    {Task.Supervised, :reply, 5, [file: 'lib/task/supervised.ex', line: 35]},
    {:proc_lib, :init_p_do_apply, 3, [file: 'proc_lib.erl', line: 249]}
  ]}
]
```

The familiar exception is still printed out, but this time we got a meaningful result. We can see that all tasks have completed successfully, except one. The crashed task returned an :exit tuple containing the error message and even a stack trace. What's more important is that our current process was isolated from the crash—you can verify this by running self() again.

It's easy to see that this is a huge improvement over our previous version. The supervisor which we introduced handles concurrent processes and errors, while we're still reaping the performance benefits of async_stream.

You may have heard of a philosophy associated with Erlang called *let it crash*. Erlang applications can quickly recover from errors by restarting parts of its system. Elixir also embraces this philosophy. Unfortunately, this approach is also frequently misunderstood. In the next section we're going to explain what *let it crash* really means and how supervisors can restart processes to make our systems even more resilient.

Understanding Let It Crash

We used Task.Supervisor to isolate a process crash, but it may seem strange we didn't prevent the crash by simply adding error handling in the send_email/1 function. In this particular case, we did this on purpose, just to simulate an unexpected exception. In practice, you should provide error handling when you expect an error to occur, and leave the rest to the supervisor as a last resort.

When discussing error handling for Elixir, the phrase *let it crash* is often used. As a result, some people assume that *let it crash* means that Erlang and Elixir developers don't do any error handling, which is not the case. Pattern matching and the with macro in Elixir make working with {:ok, result} and {:error, msg} tuples easy, and this approach is widely used in the community. Elixir also has try and rescue for catching exceptions, similar to try and catch in other languages.

However, as much as we try as engineers, we know errors can happen. This often leads to something called _defensive programming_. It describes the practice of relentlessly trying to cover every single possible scenario for failure, even when some scenarios are very unlikely to happen, and not worth dealing with.

Erlang and Elixir take a different approach to defensive programming. Since all code runs in processes and processes that are lightweight, they focus on how the system can *recover from crashes* versus how to *prevent all crashes*. You can choose to allow a part (or even the whole) of the application to crash and restart, but handle other errors yourself. This shift in thinking and software design is the reason why Erlang became famous for its reliability and scalability.

That's where supervisors come into play. We saw that supervisors can isolate crashes, but they can also restart child processes. There are three different *restart values* available to us:

- :temporary will never restart child processes.
- :transient will restart child processes but only when they exit with an error.
- :permanent always restarts children, keeping them running, even when they try to shut down without an error.

Clarification on the Terminology Used

 The word restart is slightly misleading in the context of Elixir processes. Once a process exits, it cannot be brought back to life. Therefore, restarting a process results in starting a new process to take the place of the old one, using the same child specification.

Depending on the frequency of the crash, the supervisor itself can also terminate when a child process cannot be recovered. Remember that supervisor's responsibility is to watch over its processes. If a :transient or :permanent restart value is used and a process keeps crashing, the supervisor will exit, because it has failed to restart that process. We are going to discuss this in more detail in Chapter 2, Long-Running Processes Using GenServer, on page 25.

The built-in Task.Supervisor which we used so far is already using the :temporary restart value for child processes. This is a sensible default, because it prevents all tasks processes from crashing if another task exits with an error. However, these options will come in handy in the next chapter when we start building more complex supervision trees.

Wrapping Up

Congratulations on completing this chapter! You've come a long way from running synchronous code and patiently waiting for it to complete. We covered Elixir processes and used the Task module to do work concurrently and in parallel, easily avoiding timeout errors and unexpected exceptions. You also learned about supervisors, which are the foundation of building fault-tolerant Elixir applications. A lot of the things we covered so far will appear again in the following chapters, so we have created a strong foundation to build upon.

Although the Task module is very powerful and versatile, it is only useful for running one-off functions concurrently. As a result, Task processes are short-lived and exit as soon as they complete. In the next chapter, we're going to introduce another type of process, which is capable of running and maintaining state for as long as we need it to. It is going to completely change the way you build applications forever, and this is not an exaggeration. We're also going to expand our knowledge of supervisors and start building more complex systems. Let's not waste time, and jump straight into it.

CHAPTER 2

Long-Running Processes Using GenServer

The Task module is useful for running single async functions, but as logic becomes more complex, you will need a sharper tool. In this chapter, we'll look at how to create long-lived processes that also run in the background, but offer greater control and more flexibility.

Concurrent work often takes a long time to complete, such as when you are importing a large amount of user data from another service or relying on third-party APIs, for example. This presents several challenges when using the Task module. What if an API service goes briefly offline or a network error causes the task to fail? Do you need to increase the :timeout setting because the network is slow? How do you show progress to the user and provide better user experience?

There are also times when we want to run some code in the background continuously. In a banking application, you may need the latest foreign currency exchange rates, which means periodically retrieving the data and storing it somewhere, for as long as the application runs.

These and many other problems could be solved by using a GenServer. GenServer, which is short for *generic server*, enables us to create concurrent processes that we can interact with. Just like a Web server, it listens for requests and can respond with a result. GenServer processes also have their own state, which they keep in memory until the process exits. You also have a lot more options when it comes to supervising GenServer processes and dealing with potential errors. Since GenServer is part of the OTP, it is already available for you to use in Elixir—there is no need to install any dependencies.

In this chapter, you are going to learn how to use GenServer to create stateful processes that you can interact with. We'll look at the different supervisor strategies and see how restart options work in practice. We'll tie everything together by building a simple but effective job-processing system, and you'll understand how to design fault-tolerant applications and manage processes using the Elixir Registry.

There is a lot to cover in this chapter, so let's get started!

Starting with a Basic GenServer

We are going to continue working on the sender project from the previous chapter. If you decided to skip that part, please see Creating Our Playground, on page 3 and follow the steps to create a new Elixir project and make the required change in sender.ex. We are going to create a GenServer process from scratch and see how it compares to Task processes.

First, we're going to create a new file in the lib directory. Let's name it send_ server.ex. In that file, we'll define our SendServer module like so:

```
defmodule SendServer do
  use GenServer

end
```

The use macro for the GenServer module does two things for us. First, it automatically injects the line @behaviour GenServer in our SendServer module. If you're not familiar with behaviours in Elixir, they're similar to interfaces and contracts in other programming languages. Second, it provides a default GenServer implementation for us by injecting all functions required by the GenServer behaviour.

We can verify that our code compiles by starting IEx:

```
$ iex -S mix
Compiling 3 files (.ex)
warning: function init/1 required by behaviour GenServer is not
  implemented (in module SendServer).

We will inject a default implementation for now:

    def init(init_arg) do
      {:ok, init_arg}
    end

You can copy the implementation above or define your own that converts the
  arguments given to GenServer.start_link/3 to the server state.

  lib/send_server.ex:1: SendServer (module)

Generated sender app

iex(1)>
```

You just created your first GenServer process! However, we didn't write any logic for SendServer so it doesn't do anything useful at this point. We also got a warning message by the compiler, telling us that the init/1 function is missing and was replaced by a default implementation.

The GenServer module provides default implementations for several functions required by the GenServer behaviour. These functions are known as *callbacks*, and init/1 is one of them. Callbacks are important because they allow you to customize the GenServer process by adding your own business logic to it. In the following section, you will learn about the most frequently used callbacks and some examples of how to use them.

GenServer Callbacks In Depth

The best way to learn how callbacks work is to see them in action. We are going to add some functionality to the SendServer module and introduce the most common GenServer callbacks along the way.

You can implement a callback by declaring it in the SendServer module like any other function. By doing this, you are replacing the default function that GenServer provides. This is sometimes called *overriding* the default implementation. When implementing a callback, there are two things you need to know:

- What arguments the callback function takes
- What return values are supported

We're going to cover the following callback functions for the GenServer behaviour:

- handle_call/3
- handle_cast/2
- handle_continue/2
- handle_info/2
- init/1
- terminate/2

Learning about these callbacks will enable you take full advantage of your GenServer process. There are two callbacks which we're going to skip, code_change/2 and format_status/2. We will also focus on the most frequently used return values, leaving some behind. All callbacks and return values are well documented on Elixir's HexDocs page, so feel free to go online and explore further what's possible with GenServer.

Remember the warning about the init/1 function that we saw earlier? Let's fix it by implementing the init/1 callback first.

Initializing the Process

The init/1 callback runs as soon as the process starts. When you start a GenServer process, you can optionally provide a list of arguments. This list is made available to you in the init/1 callback. This is a convenient way to provide some configuration details at runtime for the process. We mentioned that each GenServer process has its own in-memory state. This state is created by the init/1 function as well.

We are going to extend SendServer with the ability to send emails. If an email fails to send for whatever reason, we will also retry sending it, but we will limit the maximum number of retries. We will keep the business logic as simple as possible, so we can focus on learning how GenServer works.

First, let's add the following code to send_server.ex right after use GenServer:

```
def init(args) do
  IO.puts("Received arguments: #{inspect(args)}")
  max_retries = Keyword.get(args, :max_retries, 5)
  state = %{emails: [], max_retries: max_retries}
  {:ok, state}
end
```

We use the argument max_retries if present, otherwise we default to five retries max. We will also keep track of all sent emails using the emails list. These variables will be kept in the initial state for the process. Finally, the function returns {:ok, state}. This means that the process has successfully initialized.

We will cover the other possible return values in just a moment, but first, let's start SendServer to make sure it works as expected.

With the IEx shell open, run recompile() and then the following code:

```
iex> {:ok, pid} = GenServer.start(SendServer, [max_retries: 1])
```

You should see output similar to this one:

```
Received arguments: [max_retries: 1]
{:ok, #PID<0.228.0>}
```

SendServer is now running in the background. There are several ways to stop a running process, as you will see later, but for now, let's use GenServer.stop/3:

```
iex> GenServer.stop(pid)
:ok
```

There are a number of result values supported by the init/1 callback. The most common ones are:

```
{:ok, state}
{:ok, state, {:continue, term}}
:ignore
{:stop, reason}
```

We already used {:ok, state}. The extra option {:continue, term} is great for doing post-initialization work. You may be tempted to add complex logic to your init/1 function, such as fetching information from the database to populate the GenServer state, but that's not desirable because the init/1 function is synchronous and should be quick. This is where {:continue, term} becomes really useful. If you return {:ok, state, {:continue, :fetch_from_database}}, the handle_continue/2 callback will be invoked after init/1, so you can provide the following implementation:

```
def handle_continue(:fetch_from_database, state) do
  # called after init/1
end
```

We will discuss handle_continue/2 in just a moment.

Finally, the last two return values help us stop the process from starting. If the given configuration is not valid or something else prevents this process from continuing, we can return either :ignore or {:stop, reason}. The difference is that if the process is under a supervisor, {:stop, reason} will make the supervisor restart it, while :ignore won't trigger a restart.

Breaking Down Work in Multiple Steps

The handle_continue/2 callback is a recent addition to GenServer. Often GenServer processes do complex work as soon as they start. Rather than blocking the whole application from starting, we return {:ok, state, {:continue, term}} from the init/1 callback, and use handle_continue/2.

Accepted return values for handle_continue/2 include:

```
{:noreply, new_state}
{:noreply, new_state, {:continue, term}}
{:stop, reason, new_state}
```

Since the callback receives the latest state, we can use it to update it with new information by returning {:noreply, new_state}. For example:

```
def handle_continue(:fetch_from_database, state) do
  # get `users` from the database
  {:noreply, Map.put(state, :users, users)}
end
```

The other return values are similar to the ones we already covered for init/1, but it's interesting to note that handle_continue/2 can also return {:continue, term}, which will trigger another handle_continue/2. You can use this to break down work to several steps when needed. Although handle_continue/2 is often used in conjunction with init/1, other callbacks can also return {:continue, term}.

Next, we're going to see how we can communicate with the GenServer process.

Sending Process Messages

One of the highlights of GenServer processes is you can interact with them while they're still running. This is done by sending messages to the process. If you want to get some information back from the process, you use GenServer.call/3. When you don't need a result back, you can use GenServer.cast/2. Both functions accept the process identifier as their first argument, and a message to send to the process as the second argument. Messages could be any Elixir term.

When the cast/2 and call/3 functions are used, the handle_cast/2 and handle_call/3 callbacks are invoked, respectively. Let's see how they work in practice. We will implement an interface to get the current process state, as well as start sending emails.

Add the following code to send_server.ex:

```
def handle_call(:get_state, _from, state) do
  {:reply, state, state}
end
```

It is common to use pattern matching when implementing callbacks, since there could be multiple callback implementations for each type of message. For this one, we expect the message :get_state. The arguments given to handle_call/3 include the sender (which we do not use, hence the underscore _from) and the current process state.

The most common return values from handle_call/3 are:

```
{:reply, reply, new_state}
{:reply, reply, new_state, {:continue, term}}
{:stop, reason, reply, new_state}
```

By returning {reply, state, state} we send back the current state to the caller.

Let's recompile() and try it in action:

```
iex> {:ok, pid} = GenServer.start(SendServer, [max_retries: 1])
Received arguments: [max_retries: 1]
{:ok, #PID<0.265.0>}

iex> GenServer.call(pid, :get_state)
%{emails: [], max_retries: 1}
```

That's great; we can see that the current state is just as we set it up in the init/1 callback.

Now, let's implement sending emails using handle_cast/2. The arguments given to handle_cast/2 are just a term for the message and state. We're going to pattern match on the message {:send, email}:

```
def handle_cast({:send, email}, state) do
  # to do...
end
```

Most of the time you will return one of the following tuples:

```
{:noreply, new_state}
{:noreply, new_state, {:continue, term}}
{:stop, reason, new_state}
```

To refresh your memory, this is how the Sender.send_email/1 function works:

```
def send_email(email) do
  Process.sleep(3000)
  IO.puts("Email to #{email} sent")
  {:ok, "email_sent"}
end
```

Let's call the send_email/1 function from our handle_cast/2 callback, and update the process state when this happens:

```
def handle_cast({:send, email}, state) do
  Sender.send_email(email)
  emails = [%{email: email, status: "sent", retries: 0}] ++ state.emails

  {:noreply, %{state | emails: emails}}
end
```

To try out these changes, you may need to restart IEx and run the process again. Let's see if sending emails works:

```
iex(1)> {:ok, pid} = GenServer.start(SendServer, [max_retries: 1])
Received arguments: [max_retries: 1]
{:ok, #PID<0.151.0>}

iex(2)> GenServer.cast(pid, {:send, "hello@email.com"})
:ok
Email to hello@email.com sent

iex(3)> GenServer.call(pid, :get_state)
%{
  emails: [%{email: "hello@email.com", retries: 0, status: "sent"}],
  max_retries: 1
}
```

Everything seems to work just as we wanted. When using GenServer.cast/2, we always get :ok as a reply. In fact, the reply comes almost immediately. This simply means that the GenServer process has acknowledged the message, while the actual work is being performed by the process.

Notifying the Process of Events

Other than using GenServer.cast/2 and GenServer.call/3, you can also send a message to a process using Process.send/2. This type of generic message will trigger the handle_info/2 callback, which works exactly like handle_cast/2 and can return the same set of tuples. Usually handle_info/2 deals with system messages. Normally, you will expose your server API using cast/2 and call/2, and keep send/2 for internal use.

Let's see how we can use handle_info/2. We will implement retries for emails that fail to send. To test this, we need to modify sender.ex, so one of the emails returns an error. Replace your send_mail/1 logic with this:

```
def send_email("konnichiwa@world.com" = _email),
  do: :error

def send_email(email) do
  Process.sleep(3000)
  IO.puts("Email to #{email} sent")
  {:ok, "email_sent"}
end
```

Now all emails to *konnichiwa@world.com* will return :error, but we have to make sure this is persisted correctly. Next, update the handle_cast/2 callback in Send-Server:

```elixir
def handle_cast({:send, email}, state) do
  status =
    case Sender.send_email(email) do
      {:ok, "email_sent"} -> "sent"
      :error -> "failed"
    end

  emails = [%{email: email, status: status, retries: 0}] ++ state.emails

  {:noreply, %{state | emails: emails}}
end
```

Now we have everything in place to implement retries. We will use Process.send_after/3 which is similar to Process.send/2, except that it sends the message after the specified delay. We will start periodically checking for failed emails as soon as the server starts, so let's add this to our init/1 callback, before the return statement:

```elixir
Process.send_after(self(), :retry, 5000)
```

The first argument of send_after/3 is the process identifier. We use the self() function which returns the *PID* for the current process. The second argument is the name of the message, which in our case is :retry, but it could be any Elixir term. The last argument is the delay, in milliseconds, after which the message will be sent. We set this to five seconds.

Finally, let's implement handle_info/2 for the :retry message. This implementation will be a bit bigger in comparison to previous ones, but don't worry, we'll explain everything right after:

```elixir
def handle_info(:retry, state) do
  {failed, done} =
    Enum.split_with(state.emails, fn item ->
      item.status == "failed" && item.retries < state.max_retries
    end)

  retried =
    Enum.map(failed, fn item ->
      IO.puts("Retrying email #{item.email}...")

      new_status =
        case Sender.send_email(item.email) do
          {:ok, "email_sent"} -> "sent"
          :error -> "failed"
        end
```

```
      %{email: item.email, status: new_status, retries: item.retries + 1}
    end)

  Process.send_after(self(), :retry, 5000)

  {:noreply, %{state | emails: retried ++ done}}
end
```

We use Enum.split_with/2 to divide the items in the state.emails list into two categories: emails to retry, and everything else. We don't want to retry emails that were sent successfully or the ones that exceeded the max_retries setting for SendServer. The rest of the code simply iterates over the failed group of emails and attempts to resend them. We increase the retries counter after each attempt.

Finally, before we update the return and update the state, we schedule another periodic check with Process.send_after/3, so we can repeat the process.

You can now try this in IEx; just remember to use konnichiwa@world.com to test the new retry logic:

```
iex(1)> {:ok, pid} = GenServer.start(SendServer, max_retries: 2)
Received arguments: [max_retries: 2]
{:ok, #PID<0.156.0>}

iex(2)> GenServer.cast(pid, {:send, "hello@world.com"})
:ok
Email to hello@world.com sent

iex(3)> GenServer.cast(pid, {:send, "aloha@world.com"})
:ok
Email to aloha@world.com sent

iex(4)> GenServer.cast(pid, {:send, "konnichiwa@world.com"})
:ok
Retrying email konnichiwa@world.com...
Retrying email konnichiwa@world.com...

iex(5)> GenServer.call(pid, :get_state)
%{
  emails: [
    %{email: "konnichiwa@world.com", retries: 2, status: "failed"},
    %{email: "aloha@world.com", retries: 0, status: "sent"},
    %{email: "hello@world.com", retries: 0, status: "sent"}
  ],
  max_retries: 2
}
```

Great, this seems to work as expected. The process retries konnichiwa@world.com twice, before giving up. Note that when we started the process, we configured it with max_retries: 2 rather than falling back to the default value of 5. We can verify this by getting the process's state using GenServer.call/2.

Process Teardown

The final callback in the list is terminate/2. It is usually invoked before the process exits, but only when the process *itself* is responsible for the exit. Most often, the exit will result from explicitly returning {:stop, reason, state} from a callback (excluding init/1) or when an unhandled exception happens within the process.

Caution When Relying on terminate/2

 There are cases when a GenServer process is forced to exit due to an external event, for example, when the whole application shuts down. In those cases, terminate/2 will not be invoked by default. This is something you have to keep in mind if you want to ensure that important business logic always runs before the process exits. For example, you may want to persist in-memory data (stored in the process's state) to the database before the process dies.

This is out of the scope of this book, but if you want to ensure that terminate/2 is always called, look into setting Process.flag(:trap_exit, true) on the process, or use Process.monitor/1 to perform the required work in a separate process.

Let's implement terminate/2 by printing a message before the process exits:

```
def terminate(reason, _state) do
  IO.puts("Terminating with reason #{reason}")
end
```

The return value of terminate/2 is not important; you can return anything. Restart IEx and use GenServer.stop/1 to stop the process:

```
iex(1)> {:ok, pid} = GenServer.start(SendServer, [])
Received arguments: []
{:ok, #PID<0.152.0>}

iex(2)> GenServer.stop(pid)
Terminating with reason normal
:ok
```

We covered the most popular callbacks and their return values, which gives you a strong foundation to start building your own GenServer processes. We also finished building our SendServer module, which can now send and retry failed emails.

However, our SendServer implementation is far from ideal. Remember that send_email/1 pauses the process for three seconds. If you try running GenServer.cast(pid, {:send, "hello@email.com"}) several times in a row, GenServer will acknowledge all messages by returning :ok. However, it won't be able to perform the work straight away if it is busy doing something else. After all, it is just a single process doing all the work. All these messages will be put in the process's *message queue*, and executed one by one.

Even worse, if you try using GenServer.call(pid, :get_state) while the process is still busy, you will get a timeout error. By default, the GenServer.call/3 will error after 5000ms. We can tweak this by providing an optional third argument, but this is still not a practical solution.

We are going to fix this right away by building a significantly improved job-processing system. It will be capable of performing any job concurrently, such as sending emails and retrying the jobs that fail. All we have to do is change our approach slightly. Keep reading!

Using the Task Module with GenServer

 You can free up your GenServer process by using Task.start/1 and Task.async/2 to run code concurrently. Upon completion, the Task process will send messages back to GenServer, which you can process with handle_info/2. For more information, see the documentation for Task.Supervisor.async_nolink/3[2] which contains some useful examples.

Building a Job-Processing System

In the previous chapter, we used the Task module to start a new process when sending each email. We are going to adopt the same approach for our job-processing system. Rather than having a single GenServer that does all the work, we will start a GenServer process for each job. This will help us leverage concurrency and improve performance.

We also don't want to lose any features that we have introduced so far in this chapter—we want to be able to retry failed jobs and configure the process to suit our needs. Finally, we will introduce a new type of supervisor to help us manage these processes and provide fault tolerance. The figure on page 37 will give you a high-level overview of what we're going to build.

To begin, let's scaffold a new Elixir project with a supervision tree. We will call it jobber, which is not the most creative name, but it will do the job (pun intended):

```
$ mix new jobber --sup
```

Then change your current directory to jobber.

---

2. https://hexdocs.pm/elixir/Task.Supervisor.html#async_nolink/3

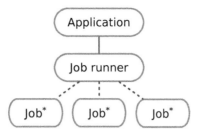

* processes started on demand

Next, we will create our GenServer process, which will do the heavy lifting. Create the file job.ex in lib/jobber with the following content:

```elixir
defmodule Jobber.Job do
  use GenServer
  require Logger

end
```

Just like we did before, we brought in the GenServer behaviour and implementation. We are also going to use Elixir's Logger module for nicer log messages.

Next, let's implement the init/1 callback and initial process configuration.

Initializing the Job Process

We are going to use a struct to keep track of the process state. Structs are just like maps, but they provide some additional features, including default values for the struct's attributes. Each job will have several fields, such as a short id to uniquely identify the process, the work function itself, and the already familiar retries and max_retries. We will also keep track of the status of each job, which will be either new, errored, failed, or done.

Add the following struct definition to job.ex:

```elixir
jobber/lib/jobber/job.ex
defstruct [:work, :id, :max_retries, retries: 0, status: "new"]
```

Next, implement the init/1 callback:

```elixir
jobber/lib/jobber/job.ex
def init(args) do
  work = Keyword.fetch!(args, :work)
  id = Keyword.get(args, :id, random_job_id())
  max_retries = Keyword.get(args, :max_retries, 3)

  state = %Jobber.Job{id: id, work: work, max_retries: max_retries}
  {:ok, state, {:continue, :run}}
end
```

The code is similar to SendServer. You may notice that we use the Keyword.fetch!/2 function here to get the work argument. This function will throw an error if you forget to provide this parameter by accident. We also generate a default id, in case an id is not available. There are different ways to generate a random identifier in Elixir. We will use Erlang's :crypto module and define random_job_id/0 like this:

```
jobber/lib/jobber/job.ex
defp random_job_id() do
  :crypto.strong_rand_bytes(5) |> Base.url_encode64(padding: false)
end
```

This will ensure that the id is unique and short at the same time, making it easy to work with. We must also add :crypto to the extra_applications list in mix.exs:

```
jobber/mix.exs
def application do
  [
    extra_applications: [:logger, :crypto],
    mod: {Jobber.Application, []}
  ]
end
```

Although the :crypto module is available to us, it is not part of the Erlang standard library, so it must be added to extra_applications when it is used.

Performing Work

We returned {:ok, state, {:continue, :run}} from the init/1 callback, so we have to handle this message next. Within the handle_continue/2 callback, we will perform the required work as soon as the process finishes initializing:

```
jobber/lib/jobber/job.ex
def handle_continue(:run, state) do
  new_state = state.work.() |> handle_job_result(state)

  if new_state.status == "errored" do
    Process.send_after(self(), :retry, 5000)
    {:noreply, new_state}
  else
    Logger.info("Job exiting #{state.id}")
    {:stop, :normal, new_state}
  end
end
```

Since the work attribute is an anonymous function, we can invoke it using the state.work.() syntax, and then process the result. We are going to use the status attribute to determine whether or not we need to retry the job again. If the status is errored, we schedule another attempt in five seconds, and keep the process running. Otherwise, for done and failed, we stop the process, as there isn't any work left to do.

We need to consider three different outcomes when handling the result:

- Success, when the job completes and returns {:ok, data}
- Initial error, when it fails the first time with :error
- Retry error, when we attempt to rerun the job and also receive :error

We will use pattern matching here, so each handle_job_result/2 function definition will handle one outcome:

```
jobber/lib/jobber/job.ex
defp handle_job_result({:ok, _data}, state) do
  Logger.info("Job completed #{state.id}")
  %Jobber.Job{state | status: "done"}
end

defp handle_job_result(:error, %{status: "new"} = state) do
  Logger.warn("Job errored #{state.id}")
  %Jobber.Job{state | status: "errored"}
end

defp handle_job_result(:error, %{status: "errored"} = state) do
  Logger.warn("Job retry failed #{state.id}")
  new_state = %Jobber.Job{state | retries: state.retries + 1}

  if new_state.retries == state.max_retries do
    %Jobber.Job{new_state | status: "failed"}
  else
    new_state
  end
end
```

The logic is again not much different compared to SendServer. However, this implementation requires that all jobs return {:ok, data} (although we ignore the data result to keep things simple) or :error. If there is more than one type of error that you want to support, you can return {:error, reason} instead, to allow for more granular error handling.

Finally, we have to implement a callback to process the :retry message. Since retrying a task is the same as running it again, we can do this:

```
jobber/lib/jobber/job.ex
def handle_info(:retry, state) do
  # Delegate work to the `handle_continue/2` callback.
  {:noreply, state, {:continue, :run}}
end
```

This will immediately trigger another :run message.

We're now ready to see how the Job process works in action. Start IEx and run a job like this:

```
iex(1)> GenServer.start(Jobber.Job, work: fn -> Process.sleep(5000);
  {:ok, []} end)

{:ok, #PID<0.261.0>}

11:35:08.221 [info]  Job completed r4Fl3I4
11:35:08.221 [info]  Job exiting r4Fl3I4
```

We used Process.sleep/1 to pretend we're doing some time-consuming work, and returned {:ok, []} as a result. Notice the semicolon before the result. We're creating an anonymous function on a single line, so we need to separate the two statements, otherwise we will get a syntax error. You can create the anonymous function beforehand to make things easier:

```
iex(2)> good_job = fn ->
...(2)> Process.sleep(5000)
...(2)> {:ok, []}
...(2)> end
#Function<21.126501267/0 in :erl_eval.expr/5>
```

You can press Enter after fn -> to continue on a new line in IEx. Now you can pass the good_job variable for the work argument directly:

```
GenServer.start(Jobber.Job, work: good_job)
```

To test the retry logic, we need a function that returns an :error. Let's create another mock function:

```
iex(3)> bad_job = fn ->
...(3)> Process.sleep(5000)
...(3)> :error
...(3)> end
#Function<21.126501267/0 in :erl_eval.expr/5>

iex(4)> GenServer.start(Jobber.Job, work: bad_job)
{:ok, #PID<0.263.0>}

11:38:49.218 [warn]  Job errored JJWXUVE
11:38:59.319 [warn]  Job retry failed JJWXUVE
11:39:09.420 [warn]  Job retry failed JJWXUVE
11:39:19.521 [warn]  Job retry failed JJWXUVE
11:39:19.521 [info]  Job exiting JJWXUVE
```

Everything is working as expected, which is good news. This is already a great improvement over SendServer, but we are not finished yet. Did you notice how we used GenServer.start/2 to start our GenServer process? This is similar to Task.start/1 in a way, in that it starts a process, without linking it to the parent process. However, if a Job process crashes due to an error, we're going to lose the process.

We can opt for using GenServer.start_link/2 instead. But now we have a different problem. The parent process will be linked, and any crash from a Job process will also propagate to the parent.

The best solution is to start all Job processes under a supervisor. The supervisor will take care of restarting the processes in the event of an error, and start jobs on demand. To accomplish this, we are going to use a new type of supervisor.

Introducing DynamicSupervisor

DynamicSupervisor is another ready-to-use supervisor available to you. It can start any GenServer process on demand. Let's add it to the supervision tree:

```
jobber/lib/jobber/application.ex
def start(_type, _args) do
  children = [
    {DynamicSupervisor, strategy: :one_for_one, name: Jobber.JobRunner},
  ]

  opts = [strategy: :one_for_one, name: Jobber.Supervisor]
  Supervisor.start_link(children, opts)
end
```

The strategy setting is required, and the only strategy that is currently accepted is :one_for_one. We will talk about supervisor strategies later in this chapter, so don't worry about this for now.

Module-Based DynamicSupervisor

 You can also define a DynamicSupervisor module, like we do later in Implementing a Supervisor, on page 45. Instead of use Supervisor you will need use DynamicSupervisor and call DynamicSupervisor.init/1 with the required :strategy value. You don't have to provide a list of children processes.

It will be useful to create some helpers for testing. Create .iex.exs at the top project directory with the following content:

```
jobber/.iex.exs
good_job = fn ->
  Process.sleep(5000)
  {:ok, []}
end

bad_job = fn ->
  Process.sleep(5000)
  :error
end
```

Predefining the test functions will save us some typing.

Next, we're going to create a helper function for starting jobs in jobber.ex:

```
jobber/lib/jobber.ex
defmodule Jobber do
  alias Jobber.{JobRunner, Job}

  def start_job(args) do
    DynamicSupervisor.start_child(JobRunner, {Job, args})
  end
end
```

Let's restart IEx and make sure everything works:

```
iex(1)> Jobber.start_job(work: good_job)
{:error,
 {:undef,
  [
    {Jobber.Job, :start_link,
     [[work: #Function<21.126501267/0 in :erl_eval.expr/5>]], []},
    {DynamicSupervisor, :start_child, 3,
     [file: 'lib/dynamic_supervisor.ex', line: 690]},
    {DynamicSupervisor, :handle_start_child, 2,
     [file: 'lib/dynamic_supervisor.ex', line: 676]},
    {:gen_server, :try_handle_call, 4, [file: 'gen_server.erl', line: 661]},
    {:gen_server, :handle_msg, 6, [file: 'gen_server.erl', line: 690]},
    {:proc_lib, :init_p_do_apply, 3, [file: 'proc_lib.erl', line: 249]}
  ]}}
```

DynamicSupervisor.start_child/2 was supposed to start a new Job process, but it failed with an error. The error message is not very clear, but the reason is that we haven't implemented a start_link/1 function in the Job module yet. DynamicSupervisor expects start_link/1 to be defined, and uses it to start the process and link it automatically. Let's add it next:

```
jobber/lib/jobber/job.ex
def start_link(args) do
  GenServer.start_link(__MODULE__, args)
end
```

This simple fix should be enough. Run recompile() in IEx and try it again. This time, the job will start successfully, but then something strange happens:

```
iex(1)> Jobber.start_job(work: good_job)
{:ok, #PID<0.163.0>}

17:02:28.773 [info]  Job completed nBSU4U0
17:02:28.780 [info]  Job exiting nBSU4U0
17:02:33.782 [info]  Job completed PkDVtBs
```

```
17:02:33.782 [info]  Job exiting PkDVtBs
17:02:38.783 [info]  Job completed Q0MS8T8
...
```

You get an endless stream of jobs being started. What could be the issue?

Process Restart Values Revisited

In the previous chapter in Understanding Let It Crash, on page 22 we talked about restart values. By default, GenServer processes are always restarted by their supervisor, which is the :permanent setting. In our case, we intentionally shut down the process. However, JobRunner thinks something must have gone wrong, so it will keep restarting the process forever. We can easily fix this by using the :transient restart option, which tells the supervisor not to restart the process if it is exiting normally. Modify our use GenServer statement in job.ex to set the new setting:

```
use GenServer, restart: :transient
```

You can quit the old IEx session and start a new one to give this a go:

```
iex(1)> Jobber.start_job(work: good_job)
{:ok, #PID<0.158.0>}

17:28:41.456 [info]  Job completed fJ1qlbo
17:28:41.456 [info]  Job exiting fJ1qlbo
```

We fixed the issue successfully. Let's try the bad_job test case:

```
iex(2)> Jobber.start_job(work: bad_job)
{:ok, #PID<0.160.0>}

14:31:14.798 [warn]  Job errored DFXanZw
14:31:24.899 [warn]  Job retry failed DFXanZw
14:31:35.000 [warn]  Job retry failed DFXanZw
14:31:45.101 [warn]  Job retry failed DFXanZw
14:31:45.101 [info]  Job exiting DFXanZw
```

So far so good, but the ultimate test is to see how the JobRunner supervisor performs when an exception happens. Exit IEx and edit .iex.exs to add a new test case function:

```
doomed_job = fn ->
  Process.sleep(5000)
  raise "Boom!"
end
```

Start the jobber app again and give the doomed_job function to JobRunner:

```
iex> Jobber.start_job(work: doomed_job)
{:ok, #PID<0.163.0>}

[error] GenServer #PID<0.163.0> terminating
** (RuntimeError) Boom!
    (stdlib 3.13) erl_eval.erl:678: :erl_eval.do_apply/6
    (jobber 0.1.0) lib/jobber/job.ex:28: Jobber.Job.handle_continue/2
    (stdlib 3.13) gen_server.erl:680: :gen_server.try_dispatch/4
    (stdlib 3.13) gen_server.erl:431: :gen_server.loop/7
    (stdlib 3.13) proc_lib.erl:226: :proc_lib.init_p_do_apply/3
Last message: {:continue, :run}

-- rest of the error log omitted --
```

The process is stuck once gain. It seems to be continuously restarting by throwing the same exception over and over again. There is one setting that we overlooked—the restart configuration on the supervisor. We will tackle this next.

Adjusting Restart Frequency

A supervisor like JobRunner has two settings—max_restarts and max_seconds—that control something we call *restart frequency*. By default, max_restarts is set to 3 and max_seconds to 5. As a result, during a five-second time window, a supervisor will attempt to restart a process three times, before it gives up.

Right now, our Process.sleep/1 call in doomed_job is set to stop the process after 5000ms. This means that the supervisor will have time for only one restart, until the five-second window expires. Since our fake function is taking a fixed amount of time to run and error, this process of restarting continues forever.

Let's increase max_seconds to thirty seconds. Go to application.ex and add the extra setting:

```
jobber/lib/jobber/application.change1.ex
def start(_type, _args) do
  job_runner_config = [
    strategy: :one_for_one,
    max_seconds: 30,
    name: Jobber.JobRunner
  ]

  children = [
    {DynamicSupervisor, job_runner_config}
  ]

  opts = [strategy: :one_for_one, name: Jobber.Supervisor]
  Supervisor.start_link(children, opts)
end
```

Start IEx again, but this time, before you try running the experiment again, let's take a note of the PID of the JobRunner process. You will see why in a second. You can use Process.whereis/1 to retrieve the process identifier using the name of the process:

```
iex(1)> Process.whereis(Jobber.JobRunner)
#PID<0.141.0>
```

Let's try running our faulty function again. You should see something like this:

```
iex(2)> Jobber.start_job(work: doomed_job)
{:ok, #PID<0.146.0>}

16:51:59.814 [error] GenServer #PID<0.146.0> terminating
** (RuntimeError) Boom!

-- rest of the error log omitted --
```

You'll see the error message above four times, because the process is restarted three times after the first exception. This may look like a success, but it's too early to celebrate. Let's check the PID for JobRunner again:

```
iex(3)> Process.whereis(Jobber.JobRunner)
#PID<0.152.0>
```

As you can see, there is a new process identifier for JobRunner, which means that the supervisor itself was restarted. Remember that supervisor's responsibility is to watch over its processes. If a :transient or :permanent restart option is used and a process keeps crashing, the supervisor will exit, because it has failed to restart that process and ensure the reliability of the system.

As a result of JobRunner exiting, any concurrent Job processes will be also terminated. Even if a single process fails to be recovered, it could endanger all other running processes. However, this can be easily fixed by adding a supervisor for each Job process, which will handle restarts and gracefully exit when its process fails.

Implementing a Supervisor

So far we have used two types of supervisors—Task.Supervisor and DynamicSupervisor. They're great because they allow you to start processes on demand. However, they are both made with a specific goal in mind, and sometimes you will need greater configurability over how the supervisor works.

This is why you will often reach for the Supervisor behaviour to create your own supervisor from scratch. In this section, we will create a supervisor using the Supervisor behaviour, and put it in front of each Job process.

We already learned supervisors can restart child processes, and we saw how the :permanent and :transient restart values work. The last setting we haven't used is :temporary. This value tells the supervisor to ignore the process and don't worry about restarting it, even when the child process exits with an error.

Our goal is to make JobRunner start an intermediary supervisor for each job, which in turn will start the actual Job process. This new supervisor will restart the Job process if needed, but will have a restart value of :temporary, so it won't cause further damage if it fails. This figure shows what the supervision tree is going to look like after we make all the changes:

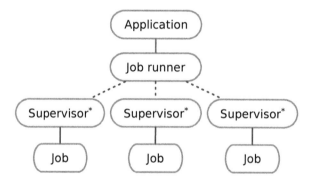

[*] processes started on demand

Let's start by creating the supervisor module:

```elixir
defmodule Jobber.JobSupervisor do
  use Supervisor, restart: :temporary

  # TODO
end
```

The use Supervisor macro is similar to use GenServer. It declares that we are implementing the Supervisor behaviour. We also make sure that this process has the :temporary restart value. Since this is going to be a linked process, we'll implement start_link/1 and init/1 next:

```elixir
jobber/lib/jobber/job_supervisor.ex
def start_link(args) do
  Supervisor.start_link(__MODULE__, args)
end

def init(args) do
  children = [
    {Jobber.Job, args}
  ]
```

```
  options = [
    strategy: :one_for_one,
    max_seconds: 30
  ]
  Supervisor.init(children, options)
end
```

These functions should look familiar to what we do when creating a GenServer, but there are some differences as well. The JobSupervisor process also takes arguments, which are handed over to the init/1 function. Then we define a list of children, which for JobSupervisor is just a single Job process. In this case, we want to pass down all configuration to the child process. Finally, instead of returning a tuple, we delegate the rest of the work to Supervisor.init/2, which will start the supervisor. If you open application.ex, you will see that the main application supervisor works the same way.

Finally, let's modify Jobber.start_job/1 to use JobSupervisor instead of running the Job process directly:

jobber/lib/jobber.change1.ex
```
defmodule Jobber do
  alias Jobber.{JobRunner, JobSupervisor}

  def start_job(args) do
    DynamicSupervisor.start_child(JobRunner, {JobSupervisor, args})
  end
end
```

We can now start IEx and repeat our last experiment:

```
iex(1)> Process.whereis(Jobber.JobRunner)
#PID<0.155.0>

iex(2)> Jobber.start_job(work: doomed_job)
{:ok, #PID<0.160.0>}
21:24:34.925 [error] GenServer #PID<0.161.0> terminating
** (RuntimeError) Boom!

-- errors omitted --

iex(3)> Process.whereis(Jobber.JobRunner)
#PID<0.155.0>
```

The JobRunner process is intact, which means that we successfully isolated potential errors. You also saw how easy it is to start building fault-tolerant applications, by thinking in processes and extending your system when needed.

However, we left one question unanswered. We used a setting called :strategy with a value of :one_for_one when creating the DynamicSupervisor and Supervisor processes. When creating a supervisor from scratch, you have the following supervisor strategies available:

- :one_for_one
- :one_for_all
- :rest_for_one

They tell the supervisor how to manage child process that fail. The one we used so far—:one_for_one—is great when each child process can be restarted independently, without impacting other sibling processes. This is in contrast to the :one_for_all strategy, which will restart *all* child processes when one of them fails. The last one, :rest_for_one, works similarly to :one_for_all, but only sibling processes started *after* the failed one will be restarted. This figure illustrates the differences between the three settings:

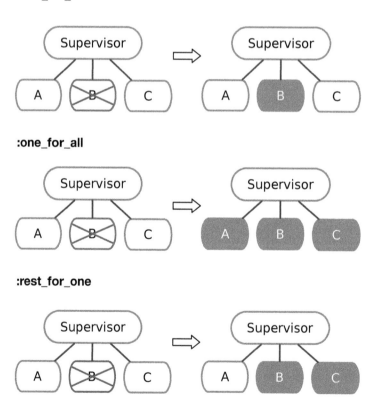

Which strategy to use depends on how your application works. You have to decide how the system should react on error, taking into consideration possible dependencies between processes.

Our job-processing system is already looking pretty good, but we are going to add one final feature. Sometimes GenServer processes could be doing intensive work, so it could be useful to limit the number of certain kind of jobs running concurrently. For example, you may want to restrict data imports from a third party system. We already support having a unique id for each Job process, so we just need to learn about process naming to make this work.

Naming Processes Using the Registry

Until now, we used the process identifier we obtained from starting the process to interact with it. However, we can optionally provide a :name value when starting a process, which can be used later on instead of a PID. This way you don't have to keep track of the PIDs of the processes you're starting. Functions like GenServer.cast/2 and GenServer.call/3 also accept a name instead of a process identifier, and you've already seen how to use Process.whereis/1 to find out the PID for JobRunner.

To make working with names easier, Elixir comes with a module called Registry. It is a very efficient key-value store with some useful functionality. Let's see how we can use it.

Processes can be named when they start via the :name option, which is what we did when creating JobRunner:

```
children = [
  {DynamicSupervisor, strategy: :one_for_one, name: Jobber.JobRunner},
]
```

Typically, the :name is set when we link a process using start_link/1. There are three types of accepted values when naming a process:

- An atom, like :job_runner. This includes module names, since they're atoms under the hood, for example, Jobber.JobRunner.

- A {:global, term} tuple, like {:global, :job_runner}, which registers the process globally. Useful for distributed applications

- A {:via, module, term} tuple, where module is an Elixir module that would take care of the registration process, using the value term

Using Elixir atoms may seem convenient, but could be a problem when starting many uniquely named process, like we do for jobber. Atoms are not garbage collected by the Erlang VM, and there are soft limits on how many atoms could be used in the system.

This is where the Elixir Registry comes in. It allows us to use strings, rather than atoms, which don't have the same limitation and are generally much easier to work with. The Registry also comes with some helpers for looking up process by name and filtering the results, which are nice additions.

Each Registry works as a process which you have to include in your application supervision tree. You can even start multiple registries if you want to. We are going to create a new Registry next, then use it for registering Job processes dynamically.

Starting a Registry Process

Creating and starting a registry is easy. Make the following change to application.ex:

```
jobber/lib/jobber/application.change2.ex
def start(_type, _args) do
  job_runner_config = [
    strategy: :one_for_one,
    max_seconds: 30,
    name: Jobber.JobRunner
  ]

  children = [
    {Registry, keys: :unique, name: Jobber.JobRegistry},
    {DynamicSupervisor, job_runner_config}
  ]

  opts = [strategy: :one_for_one, name: Jobber.Supervisor]
  Supervisor.start_link(children, opts)
end
```

You can see that adding a Registry is similar to adding other processes. Using the :name argument, we set the name of the process to Jobber.JobRegistry. We also used the :keys setting. The keys are the names of the processes we are going to register. Using this setting, we can enforce all keys to be either :unique or allow duplicates with :duplicate. We set the value to :unique.

You can restart IEx, and the JobRegistry process will be available for you to use. Next, let's change our Job process so it uses the Registry when starting up.

Registering New Processes

We are going to make a few changes to job.ex. First, let's add a helper function, via/2, to job.ex:

```
jobber/lib/jobber/job.change1.ex
defp via(key, value) do
  {:via, Registry, {Jobber.JobRegistry, key, value}}
end
```

This will return a tuple that conforms to the required naming specification. The format is always {:via, Registry, config}, where config is also a tuple and can be either {registry_process, key} or {registry_process, key, value}. We will use the extra value element to store some useful metadata about the process. We will label each job with a type description to make it easier to find out which process is doing what.

You can use the provided id, or generate one, for the name of the process. Let's move some of the existing logic in start_link/1:

jobber/lib/jobber/job.change1.ex
```
def start_link(args) do
  args =
    if Keyword.has_key?(args, :id) do
      args
    else
      Keyword.put(args, :id, random_job_id())
    end

  id = Keyword.get(args, :id)
  type = Keyword.get(args, :type)

  GenServer.start_link(__MODULE__, args, name: via(id, type))
end
```

We've added an extra :name argument to GenServer.start_link/2 to name the process. This is where we have to provide the :via tuple, generated by the via/2 helper function. We're also passing down the :type argument, which we're going to use later.

We no longer need to generate a new id in the init/1 function, since this is now done in start_link/2. Let's update this:

jobber/lib/jobber/job.change1.ex
```
def init(args) do
  work = Keyword.fetch!(args, :work)
  id = Keyword.get(args, :id)
  max_retries = Keyword.get(args, :max_retries, 3)

  state = %Jobber.Job{id: id, work: work, max_retries: max_retries}
  {:ok, state, {:continue, :run}}
end
```

This is all we need to register the process using JobRegistry. Now we can start using the data stored in the registry to put a limit on certain jobs.

Querying the Registry

The Registry module gives you a handy function—select/2. This function uses a matching syntax from Erlang, so it looks a bit cryptic at first. However, once you understand the basic elements of it, you'll have no problem using it.

Let's add a helper function to jobber.ex to retrieve all running processes labeled with import. Then we will break it down and explain what it does:

```
jobber/lib/jobber.change2.ex
def running_imports() do
  match_all = {:"$1", :"$2", :"$3"}
  guards = [{:"==", :"$3", "import"}]
  map_result = [%{id: :"$1", pid: :"$2", type: :"$3"}]
  Registry.select(Jobber.JobRegistry, [{match_all, guards, map_result}])
end
```

Registry.select/2 takes a registry process as its first argument, and a list of match specifications as the last argument. The match specification we have is a bit lengthy, so we have broken it down to three variables:

- match_all is a wildcard that matches all entries in the registry.

- guards is a filter that filters results by the third element in the tuple, which has to be equal to "import".

- map_result is transforming the result by creating a list of maps, assigning each element of the tuple to a key, which makes the result a bit more readable.

Each value in the Registry is a tuple in the form of {name, pid, value}. In our case, name is the id, and value is the type label. Each element in the tuple is given a special identifier based on its position in the tuple. So :"$1" corresponds to the first element, which is the id, :"$2" is the pid, and so on. We use these as template variables to match, filter, and map entries in the Registry.

Let's see this in action. Go to .iex.exs and increase the timer for Process.sleep/1 on good_job:

```
good_job = fn ->
  Process.sleep(60_000)
  {:ok, []}
end
```

The function will now take one minute to complete, giving us more time to test things properly. Next, restart IEx for the changes to take effect. We will run three concurrent jobs, and two of them will be import jobs:

```
iex(1)> Jobber.start_job(work: good_job, type: "import")
{:ok, #PID<0.161.0>}
```

```
iex(2)> Jobber.start_job(work: good_job, type: "send_email")
{:ok, #PID<0.165.0>}
```

```
iex(3)> Jobber.start_job(work: good_job, type: "import")
{:ok, #PID<0.168.0>}
```

Running Jobber.running_imports() should produce something similar to this:

```
iex(4)> Jobber.running_imports()
[
  %{id: "oNnA3I8", pid: #PID<0.161.0>, type: "import"},
  %{id: "OtHGZ6A", pid: #PID<0.168.0>, type: "import"}
]
```

We now have a way to query JobRegistry and limit concurrency for import jobs.

Learning About Match Specifications

To learn more about match specifications for Registry.select/2, which are also useful when working with ETS, you can check the official Elixir documentation on HexDocs.[3] If you want to dig deeper, Erlang's match specification guide[4] is the best reference on the topic.

Limiting Concurrency of Import Jobs

We are going to put our new running_imports/0 to use. Let's add this check to Jobber.start_job/1:

```
jobber/lib/jobber.change2.ex
def start_job(args) do
  if Enum.count(running_imports()) >= 5 do
    {:error, :import_quota_reached}
  else
    DynamicSupervisor.start_child(JobRunner, {JobSupervisor, args})
  end
end
```

Try starting more than five jobs. After the fifth attempt, you should see this error result:

```
iex(6)> Jobber.start_job(work: good_job, type: "import")
{:error, :import_quota_reached}
```

---

3.   https://hexdocs.pm/elixir/Registry.html#select/2
4.   http://erlang.org/doc/apps/erts/match_spec.html

We have successfully enforced a limit on how many import jobs can run at any given time. We also demonstrated how you can register and lookup processes using the Registry, including adding metadata to each registered process. You can use this in a variety of ways to efficiently manage a large number of processes at runtime.

Our job-processing system is now complete. We're going to leave jobber here, but if you'd like to continue working on it, there are many other features you can consider adding, such as job queues or database persistence. You can use this project as a playground to continue practicing building fault-tolerant systems with GenServer and supervisors.

Before we wrap up, we're going to briefly cover a few functions which may come in handy when working with complex supervision trees.

Inspecting Supervisors at Runtime

When you have a supervision tree up and running, you may want to get some information from it at runtime. For example, how many processes are currently running under a particular supervisor, what kind of processes they are, and so on. In this section, we'll cover two functions that will help you answer any questions you may have about the state of the supervision tree.

The first function is count_children/1, and is available in both DynamicSupervisor and Supervisor modules. It gives us information about the number of processes currently running under the given supervisor. When you call count_children/1 with a PID or a name of a supervisor process, you will get a map with the following keys and values:

- :supervisors with total number of supervisor child processes, both active and inactive

- :workers with total number of worker (non-supervisor) child processes, both active and inactive

- :specs with the total number of all child processes, both active and inactive

- :active with the total number of actively running child processes

Let's start the jobber application with iex -S mix and try it out:

```
iex(1)> DynamicSupervisor.count_children(Jobber.JobRunner)
%{active: 0, specs: 0, supervisors: 0, workers: 0}
```

Since we just started the application, all values for JobRunner are zero. Let's create a new job and wait for it to complete. Then, run count_children/1 again:

```
iex(2)> Jobber.start_job(work: good_job)
{:ok, #PID<0.152.0>}

17:19:23.424 [info]  Job completed acBcRek
17:19:23.426 [info]  Job exiting acBcRek

iex(3)> DynamicSupervisor.count_children(Jobber.JobRunner)
%{active: 1, specs: 1, supervisors: 1, workers: 0}
```

You may be surprised to see that the value of :active is 1, even though the job process has already completed. The value of :supervisors is also 1, which means that this running process is a supervisor.

We can get more information about running child processes by using which_children/1. This function returns a list of tuples, and each tuple has four elements:

- The id of the child process, which could be :undefined for dynamically started processes

- The PID of the child process or the value :restarting when the process is in the middle of a restart

- The type of process, either :worker or :supervisor

- The module implementation, which is returned in a list

Just like count_children/1, which_children/1 is also implemented in the DynamicSupervisor and Supervisor modules.

Let's learn more about the process that is still running:

```
iex(4)> DynamicSupervisor.which_children(Jobber.JobRunner)
[{:undefined, #PID<0.152.0>, :supervisor, [Jobber.JobSupervisor]}]
```

Mystery solved—it's the JobSupervisor which was responsible for starting the Job process. This process is now running idle, since its only child process has exited successfully. We can verify this by using Supervisor.count_children/1 with the PID of the running JobSupervisor, like so:

```
iex(5)> children = DynamicSupervisor.which_children(Jobber.JobRunner)
[{:undefined, #PID<0.152.0>, :supervisor, [Jobber.JobSupervisor]}]

iex(6)> {_, pid, _, _} = List.first(children)
{:undefined, #PID<0.152.0>, :supervisor, [Jobber.JobSupervisor]}

iex(7)> Supervisor.count_children(pid)
%{active: 0, specs: 1, supervisors: 0, workers: 1}
```

As expected, there are zero active processes for this supervisor.

As you have learned already, processes are lightweight, and idle processes like JobSupervisor are unlikely to cause any issues. However, thanks to which_children/1 and count_children/1, you can easily find those processes and stop them if you wish. You can stop a supervisor using Supervisor.stop/1:

```
iex(8)> Supervisor.stop(pid)
:ok
```

If you run DynamicSupervisor.which_children(Jobber.JobRunner), you'll now get an empty list value, since there are no more active processes.

Now it's time to wrap up and do a recap.

Wrapping Up

Completing this chapter was not an easy challenge, so well done! Learning how to use GenServer correctly will open the doors to building highly concurrent and performant applications, without the complexity you've seen in other programming languages. GenServer is a versatile tool and you will reach for it often when doing work concurrently.

In this chapter, you learned about the most common callbacks used when implementing the GenServer behaviour. You saw how to use each callback, interact with the process while it's still running, and use the process state. You can start processes at runtime using DynamicSupervisor, or build your own supervisor when needed. Finally, you saw how the Registry can make registering and managing even large numbers of running processes a breeze.

The last thing we added to our job-processing system was the ability to limit concurrency. This is because running a high volume of concurrent jobs can potentially overwhelm our system, especially when the work requires a lot of system resources. In the next chapter, rather than limiting concurrency, we are going to see how to manage back-pressure and keep workload under control, while maximizing performance at the same time.

CHAPTER 3

Data-Processing Pipelines with GenStage

In previous chapters, we covered several approaches to executing data asynchronously. Although different in their own way, they had one thing in common: we were deciding the amount of work that had to be done and Elixir would then eagerly process the work to give us the result.

This has some potential drawbacks. For example, we have a finite amount of memory and CPU power available. This means that our server may become overwhelmed by the amount of work it needs to do and become slow or unresponsive. Often we rely on third-party API services, which have rate limiting in place and fixed quotas for the number of requests we can make. If we go over their quota, requests will be blocked and our application will stop working as expected.

In a nutshell, as the amount of work we need to do grows, there is an increasing chance that we can hit a certain limit on a resource available to us. You can spend more money on computer hardware or buy more powerful virtual machines, but that's usually a temporary solution that often leads to diminishing returns. For that reason, making the best use of existing resources should be a priority when designing and scaling software applications.

In this chapter, we're going to learn how to build data-processing pipelines that can utilize our system resources reliably and effectively. We'll introduce the GenStage Elixir library and the fundamental building blocks that it provides. First we are going to create a simple data-processing pipeline to start with, then scale it and extend it to demonstrate how you can tackle more complex use cases.

But before we get into it, first we need to explain what *back-pressure* is, and how it enables us to build data-processing pipelines. Let's get started!

Understanding Back-Pressure

Imagine you're a famous writer giving autographs at a book event. There is a crowd of people rushing to meet you. You can only do one autograph at a time, so the organizers let people in one by one. When you sign someone's book, you ask for the next person to come forward. What if the organizers suddenly let everyone in? Of course, it will be complete chaos! You'll try to sign everyone's books as quickly as you can, but soon you'll get stressed and exhausted, leaving the event early.

It is much more efficient to have an orderly queue of people and to take your time to sign each book. Because you always ask for the next person to come forward, you are in control of the amount of work you have to do, and it is much easier to keep going. Maybe you won't get that tired, so you decide to stay at the event longer and make sure everyone gets an autograph. This is in fact an example of handling back-pressure in real life.

How does this translate in programming? Using the GenStage library we are going to build a data-processing pipeline that works like the well-organized book event we just described. The system will process only the amount of work it can handle at a given time, just like the famous writer from our example. If the system has free capacity, it will politely ask for more work and wait for it.

This simple shift in our thinking is very powerful. It enables us to build complex data pipelines that regulate themselves to utilize the available resources in the best possible way.

Borrowing Terminology

The term *back-pressure*, according to Wikipedia, originates from fluid dynamics and the automotive industry, where it is used to describe resistance to the normal flow of fluids in pipes.

Software engineers borrowed the term and loosely use it in the context of data processing, when something is slowing down or stopping the flow of data. When we talk about using back-pressure, we actually mean using a mechanism to control or handle back-pressure in a beneficial way.

Introducing GenStage

GenStage was originally developed by José Valim, the creator of Elixir, and released in July 2016. As he described it in the official announcement:

"GenStage is a new Elixir behaviour for exchanging events with back-pressure between Elixir processes."

In the previous chapter, we used the GenServer behaviour to build long-running *server* processes. The GenStage behaviour, as its name suggests, is used to build *stages*. Stages are also Elixir processes and they're our building blocks for creating data-processing pipelines.

Stages are simple but very powerful. They can receive *events* and use them to do some useful work. They can also send events to the next stage in the pipeline. You can do that by connecting stages to each other, creating something like a chain, as you can see here:

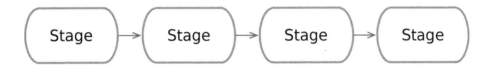

A stage can also have multiple instances of itself. Since stages are processes, this effectively means running more than one process of the same stage type. This means that you can also create something that looks like this:

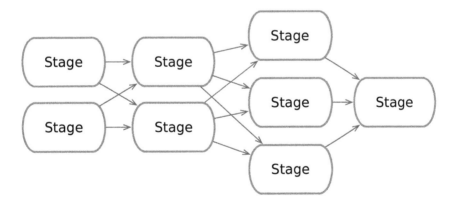

These are just two possible designs. In practice, different problems require different solutions, so your data-processing pipeline could end up looking completely different. When you finish this chapter, you will have a solid understanding of GenStage and you will be able to come up with a solution that works best for you.

As you can see, stages are very flexible and can be used in a variety of ways. However, their most important feature is back-pressure.

Although events move between stages from left to right on our diagram, it is actually the last stage in the pipeline that controls the flow. This is because the *demand* for more events travels in the opposite direction—from right to left. This figure shows how it works:

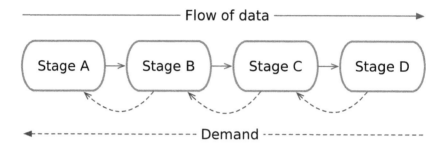

Stage D has to request events from Stage C, and so on, until the demand reaches the beginning of the pipeline. As a rule, a stage will send demand for events only when it has the capacity to receive more. When a stage gets too busy, demand will be delayed until the stage is free, slowing down the flow of data. Sounds familiar? This is exactly how the book event example from Understanding Back-Pressure, on page 58 would work if we implemented it as a data-processing pipeline. This figure illustrates how we can model the book event using stages:

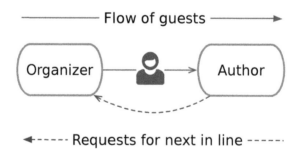

By treating guests as a flow of events, the author stage can "process" a guest by signing their book, and then request the next guest from the organizer when ready. The organizer stage, on the other hand, has to make sure that only one guest at a time comes forward, as the author requests. This is how back-pressure works in GenStage, and the best part is that you benefit from it simply by thinking in stages and connecting them together.

Connecting stages is easy, but first you need to know what stages to use. There are three different types of stages available to us: producer, consumer, and producer-consumer. Each one plays a certain role. Let's briefly cover each type of stage and see how it is made to work with the rest.

The Producer

At the beginning of a data-processing pipeline there is always a producer stage, since the producer is the source of data that flows into the pipeline. It is responsible for producing *events* for all other stages that follow. An *event* is simply something that you wish to use later on; it could be a map or a struct. You can use any valid Elixir data type. Here is an example of a two-stage data pipeline:

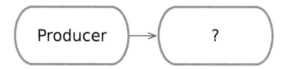

The events produced by the producer have to be processed by another stage, which is missing in the figure. What we need here is a consumer for those events.

The Consumer

Events created by the producer are received by the consumer stage. A consumer has to *subscribe* to a producer to let them know they're available, and request events.

This producer and consumer relationship is around us every day. For example, when you go to the farmer's market, the farmers that grow vegetables are producers. They wait until a customer (a consumer) comes and asks to buy some vegetables.

Consumer stages are always found at the end of the pipeline. Now we can fill in the missing process. The following figure illustrates the simplest data pipeline we can create using GenStage:

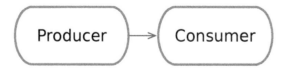

It has just a single producer and a consumer.

The Producer-Consumer

Although having a producer and a consumer is already very useful, sometimes we need to have more than two stages in our pipeline. This is where the producer-consumer stage comes in—it has the special ability to produce and consume events at the same time. The following figure shows how one or more producer-consumer stages can be used to extend a pipeline.

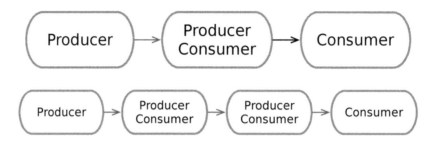

A useful analogy to a producer-consumer is the restaurant. A restaurant serves meals (producer) but in order to cook the meals, it needs ingredients sourced from its suppliers (acting as a consumer). In a nutshell, producer-consumers are the middle-man in our data-processing pipelines.

We've covered a lot of theory, so let's finally dive into some examples.

Building Your Data-Processing Pipeline

Complex use cases may require a data-processing pipeline with a consumer stage, one or more producers, and several producer-consumers in between. However, the main principles stay the same, so we're going to start with a two-stage pipeline first and demonstrate how that works.

We will build a fake service that scrapes data from web pages—normally an intensive task, dependent on system resources and a reliable network connection. Our goal is to be able to request a number of URLs to be scraped, and have the data pipeline take care of the workload.

First, let's create a new application with a supervision tree like we've done before. We will name it scraper and pretend we're going to scrape data from web pages.

```
$ mix new scraper --sup
```

This will print the usual information in the console. Let's navigate in the new directory and edit mix.exs to add gen_stage as dependency:

```
scraper/mix.exs
defp deps do
  [
    {:gen_stage, "~> 1.0"}
  ]
end
```

Next, run the command `mix do deps.get, compile` to download and compile all dependencies.

Let's add a dummy function to scraper.ex which will simulate doing some time-consuming work:

```
scraper/lib/scraper.ex
def work() do
  # For simplicity, this function is
  # just a placeholder and does not contain
  # real scraping logic.
  1..5
  |> Enum.random()
  |> :timer.seconds()
  |> Process.sleep()
end
```

The work/0 function will take a random number from one to five, convert it from seconds to milliseconds using Erlang's :timer.seconds/1 and then pass it to Process. sleep/1, pausing the process for that amount of time. As a result, calling this function will pause the current process from one to five seconds at random.

Now, let's create our producer.

Creating a Producer

Our scraper will scrape data from web pages. At the beginning of our pipeline we will put a producer stage that will be responsible for what web pages we are going to scrape. In other words, it will *produce* URLs for consumers interested in getting web pages to scrape.

We are going to name our producer PageProducer and define it in a new file page_producer.ex in the lib directory:

```
scraper/lib/page_producer.ex
defmodule PageProducer do
  use GenStage
  require Logger

  def start_link(_args) do
    initial_state = []
    GenStage.start_link(__MODULE__, initial_state, name: __MODULE__)
  end
```

```elixir
  def init(initial_state) do
    Logger.info("PageProducer init")
    {:producer, initial_state}
  end

  def handle_demand(demand, state) do
    Logger.info("PageProducer received demand for #{demand} pages")
    events = []
    {:noreply, events, state}
  end
end
```

The code above looks similar to a GenServer process code. Instead of use GenServer there is use GenStage. There is a start_link/1 function and an init/1 function. Of course there are some differences, too.

The init/1 function for GenStage processes must specify what type of stage the process is. Since we want to create a producer, we return {:producer, initial_state}. The first element in the tuple—the stage type—could be :producer, :consumer, or :producer_consumer; the second is the argument that sets the initial state for the process.

We are also implementing a handle_demand/2 callback, which you haven't seen before. This callback is required for processes of type :producer and :producer_consumer. When a :consumer process asks for events, handle_demand/2 will be invoked with two parameters: the number of events requested by the consumers and the internal state of the producer. In the result tuple, the second element must be a list containing the actual events. Right now we are just returning an empty list, but we will revisit this part later.

Creating a Consumer

Now that there is a producer in place, let's create a consumer. Since we name our producer PageProducer, we are going to call the consumer PageConsumer. Create the file page_consumer.ex and place it in the same lib directory.

scraper/lib/page_consumer.ex
```elixir
defmodule PageConsumer do
  use GenStage
  require Logger

  def start_link(_args) do
    initial_state = []
    GenStage.start_link(__MODULE__, initial_state)
  end

  def init(initial_state) do
    Logger.info("PageConsumer init")
    {:consumer, initial_state, subscribe_to: [PageProducer]}
  end
```

```
  def handle_events(events, _from, state) do
    Logger.info("PageConsumer received #{inspect(events)}")

    # Pretending that we're scraping web pages.
    Enum.each(events, fn _page ->
      Scraper.work()
    end)

    {:noreply, [], state}
  end
end
```

The code looks familiar and somewhat similar to a producer. What has changed is the atom returned by init/1, specifying the stage type. This time we are returning :consumer.

We also return some options from the init/1 function. We are telling this consumer to *subscribe* to PageProducer, via subscribe_to: [PageProducer]. This is how stages are linked together.

Since consumers receive events, we have to implement a special callback for stages of type :consumer and :producer_consumer, and this is the handle_events/3 callback. When a consumer asks for events, and the producer responds, the list of events given to a consumer will be the first parameter in the handle_events/3 function. This is where we would do something with the events and use it in a meaningful way. For now, we're just going to call our Scraper.work/1 dummy function.

Subscribing at Runtime

 You can programmatically subscribe to a producer at runtime using sync_subscribe/3 and async_subscribe/3 from the GenStage module. This is useful when consumers and/or producers are created dynamically at runtime. Note that you will also have to handle the resubscribe yourself if the producer crashes and is restarted.

Now that we have a producer and a consumer, let's add them to our application supervision tree in application.ex. Our start/2 function should look like so:

scraper/lib/scraper/application.ex
```
def start(_type, _args) do
  children = [
    PageProducer,
    PageConsumer
  ]

  opts = [strategy: :one_for_one, name: Scraper.Supervisor]
  Supervisor.start_link(children, opts)
end
```

Here we are introducing another type of child specification. This format is the shortest, and is equivalent to this:

```
children = [
  {PageProducer, []},
  {PageConsumer, []}
]
```

We are going to use this format when we don't need to pass any options to the process we are adding.

Running the app with iex -S mix should produce this:

```
19:28:18.351 [info]  PageProducer init
19:28:18.359 [info]  PageConsumer init
19:28:18.359 [info]  PageProducer received demand for 1000 pages
```

It seems that the producer and consumer are talking to each other—success. However, there are two issues: first, the producer doesn't actually produce anything (yet), and second, the consumer asked for a whopping 1000 pages. Let's tackle the issues in reverse order.

Understanding Consumer Demand

You saw that PageProducer was asked for 1000 events and you may wonder where the number comes from. By default, stages of type :consumer and :producer_consumer make sure that demand for new events is between 500 and 1000. You can configure this through the min_demand and max_demand settings. When a consumer subscribes to a producer in the init/1 function, you can pass a tuple with some configuration options:

```
# `subscribe_to` options can be a list of tuples.
sub_opts = [{PageProducer, min_demand: 500, max_demand: 1000}]
{:consumer, initial_state, subscribe_to: sub_opts}
```

By configuring demand you can control two things: max_demand will set the maximum number of events the consumer can ask for, and min_demand will determine the lowest number of events available to the consumer before it can ask for more.

The consumer is greedy and will immediately demand 1000 events on start, according to the max_demand value you set. Let's say the producer supplies 1000 events. The consumer will process the first batch using a simple formula:

```
events to process = max_demand - min_demand
```

This is to ensure that while the consumer is processing the events, fresh demand is issued to the producer to keep it busy supplying the next batch of events.

Since max_demand is 1000 and min_demand is 500 by default, the consumer will process 500 events first, and then the remaining 500, according to the formula. This means that the handle_events/3 callback will be called with a list of 500 events initially, followed by another 500 when it is done processing the previous one. The final outstanding demand for the producer will be 500 events, as shown in this figure:

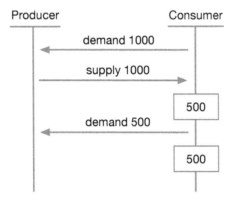

Let's take another example with the same settings. This time the producer responds with 600 events, even though the consumer asked for 1000. According to the formula, the 600 events will be broken down to batches of 500 and 100. While the consumer is processing the first batch of 500 events, there is still an outstanding demand for 400 events from the initial request. As soon as the consumer starts processing the first batch, it will ask for 500 events more. This will bring total consumer demand to 900 events. This figure illustrates the example:

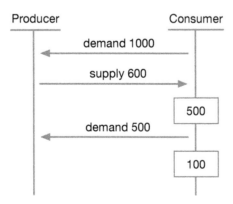

This sounds complicated and confusing at first, especially since we are dealing with concurrent processes, but there are good reasons behind this implementation. By tracking the number of events a consumer processes and number of events in progress, GenStage optimizes the flow of data for peak efficiency, keeping both consumers and producers busy at all time. The consumer demands more events only when a batch has been processed, so if the processing of the events takes longer, demand will be delayed. The opposite is also true—if events are quick to process, demand will be issued sooner. In all cases, demand will be kept within the given min_demand and max_demand values and will be constantly adjusted to fit this range by GenStage.

You don't have to always process events in batches. If you lower the value of max_demand to 1, the events will be requested one by one. Depending on your use case, you have to come up with the configuration that works best for you. The default values of 500 and 1000 are simply there to get you started. This could be challenging, so here's a simple questionnaire that will give you a good starting point:

- How long does it take to process a single event vs. 100 vs. 1000?

  - This will help you determine if it is faster to demand a batch of events, and what batch size (as opposing to one by one).

- How often do you expect new events?

  - If the producer produces events frequently and they're in constant supply, it may be beneficial to increase min_demand, especially when working in batches is ideal.

- Can processing be delayed?

  - Since consumers will wait until min_demand is satisfied by the producer, you will want to lower min_demand or even set it to 0 (demanding an event as soon as it is available by the producer).

- What system resources are available to me?

  - You can distribute the load by lowering min_demand and max_demand, buffering events, or using several consumers (more about these later).

Answering these questions should help you get started with your own GenStage implementation. It may also take you more than one attempt to find the best min_demand and max_demand strategy, so don't despair. It is always a good idea to measure how your pipeline performs and tweak the demand until you're happy with the results.

Now, for our scraper project, let's lower the demand to something more suitable:

```
scraper/lib/page_consumer.change1.ex
def init(initial_state) do
  Logger.info("PageConsumer init")
  sub_opts = [{PageProducer, min_demand: 0, max_demand: 3}]
  {:consumer, initial_state, subscribe_to: sub_opts}
end
```

With min_demand set to 0 and max_demand set to 3, we are ensuring that the consumer will take at least one event when it is available, up to three at a time. However, our producer still has to supply the consumers with events, and right now it doesn't do anything. Let's fix this.

Revisiting the Producer

Going back to PageProducer, we have implemented the handle_demand/2 callback to respond to demand and produce events. Remember that handle_demand/2 is always called when the producer receives demand from a consumer. Since consumers always demand events when they're free, this callback will be useful when we want to respond to consumer demand immediately and keep consumers busy.

Instead, we would like to expose an API which developers can use to request pages to be scraped. In this particular use case, consumers will have to wait patiently until work is available for them. Therefore, handle_demand/2 won't be very useful for what we're trying to achieve.

Thankfully, there are several ways for a producer to dispatch events. In fact, most callbacks for :producer and :producer_consumer stages have the ability to do so.

Earlier we mentioned that GenStage is built on top of GenServer. This means that the callbacks we covered in GenServer Callbacks In Depth, on page 27 are also available for GenStage processes:

- handle_call/3
- handle_cast/2
- handle_info/3

They will be called when you invoke GenStage.call/3, GenStage.cast/2, or Process.send/3, respectively. However, the return signatures of those callbacks have an important difference to their GenServer counterparts. Here are two examples of return tuples allowed for GenStage:

```
{:reply, reply, [event], new_state}
{:noreply, [event], new_state}
```

Notice the extra element in the tuple that holds a list of event values. These callbacks work exactly the same as the handle_demand/3 callback. This is great news, because it gives us a lot of flexibility when dispatching events.

Let's implement our API in PageProducer:

scraper/lib/page_producer.change1.ex

```elixir
def scrape_pages(pages) when is_list(pages) do
  GenStage.cast(__MODULE__, {:pages, pages})
end

def handle_cast({:pages, pages}, state) do
  {:noreply, pages, state}
end
```

We have exposed a function scrape_pages/1 which accepts a list of URLs. This function will be our user-facing API. Inside the function, we call GenStage.cast/2, just like we did with GenServer before.

In the handle_cast/2 callback function, we return a tuple as a result. The first element in the tuple is always the type of reply, which is :noreply in this case. The second element must be a list, containing the events we want to dispatch. We are going to return pages, which contains our list of strings. Finally, the third element is the process state, which you can update if you need to. Here, we are just returning it unchanged. As you can see, the return tuple format is very similar to the one for GenServer, but with the addition of the events element.

Let's run our application again using the IEx shell:

```
$ iex -S mix
```

You should see an output similar to this:

```
Erlang/OTP 21 [erts-10.0.3] [source] [64-bit] [smp:4:4] [ds:4:4:10]
  [async-threads:1] [hipe] [dtrace]

Compiling 1 file (.ex)

16:10:30.437 [info]  PageProducer init
16:10:30.443 [info]  PageConsumer init
16:10:30.443 [info]  PageProducer received demand for 3 pages

Interactive Elixir (1.8.1) - press Ctrl+C to exit (type h() ENTER for help)

iex(1)>
```

As expected, the consumer sends demand as soon as it is initialized. Since our handle_demand/2 callback does not return events, this initial demand is not satisfied and therefore the consumer will wait until events are available.

Now, we're going to create a list of URLs and call our API:

```
iex(1)> pages = [
...(1)> "google.com",
...(1)> "facebook.com",
...(1)> "apple.com",
...(1)> "netflix.com",
...(1)> "amazon.com"
...(1)> ]
["google.com", "facebook.com", "apple.com", "netflix.com", "amazon.com"]

iex(2)> PageProducer.scrape_pages(pages)
```

Let's look closely at the output log:

```
16:19:51.733 [info]  PageConsumer received ["google.com",
  "facebook.com", "apple.com"]
16:20:02.742 [info]  PageProducer received demand for 1 pages
16:20:02.743 [info]  PageConsumer received ["netflix.com", "amazon.com"]
```

We can see that PageConsumer immediately received the first three pages, which took a bit of time to process, judging by the timestamps. Since only two pages were available next, our consumer realized that it has capacity for one more page, so it immediately issued demand for another page, while starting work on the other two. That's great, everything is working as expected.

Congratulations, you just created your first data-processing pipeline with GenStage! We have created a producer and a consumer, put them to work together and introduced a lot of new concepts on the way.

However, we are not finished with our scraper project just yet. Although it is working correctly, we can in fact easily improve it with just a few small changes. Since our Scrape.work/0 function is very slow, working in batches and scraping pages in a sequence is not ideal. We can significantly improve performance by taking advantage of modern multi-core CPUs to scrape pages concurrently. Let's see how that works.

Adding More Consumers

Rather than working in batches within a single process, we can easily scale our data-processing pipeline by running more than one consumer, each responsible for scraping one page at a time. To do this, let's adjust PageConsumer's demand:

```
scraper/lib/page_consumer.change2.ex
def init(initial_state) do
  Logger.info("PageConsumer init")
  sub_opts = [{PageProducer, min_demand: 0, max_demand: 1}]
  {:consumer, initial_state, subscribe_to: sub_opts}
end
```

and add another PageConsumer to our supervision tree:

```
scraper/lib/scraper/application.change1.ex
children = [
  PageProducer,
➤  Supervisor.child_spec(PageConsumer, id: :consumer_a),
➤  Supervisor.child_spec(PageConsumer, id: :consumer_b)
]
```

Now our consumer will take only one event at a time, but we have two consumer processes running concurrently. As soon as one is free, it will issue demand to scrape another page.

Notice that when we added another PageConsumer, we used Supervisor.child_spec/2. As we saw, each process should have a unique ID in the supervision tree. In the example above, the processes are called :consumer_a and :consumer_b. If we do not do that, we will get an error as soon as the main supervisor initializes. We can also use the Registry module to assign a name to each process, as we have done in Naming Processes Using the Registry, on page 49.

With this approach, we can add as many consumer processes as needed and GenServer will distribute the events for us, acting as a load balancer. Let's try the scrape_pages/1 function again and compare the results:

```
16:44:58.617 [info]  PageConsumer received ["facebook.com"]
16:44:58.617 [info]  PageConsumer received ["google.com"]
16:45:01.618 [info]  PageConsumer received ["apple.com"]
16:45:02.618 [info]  PageConsumer received ["netflix.com"]
16:45:02.619 [info]  PageConsumer received ["amazon.com"]
16:45:05.620 [info]  PageProducer received demand for 1 pages
16:45:06.619 [info]  PageProducer received demand for 1 pages
```

If you look closely at the timestamps, you can see how the first two pages were immediately picked up by the waiting consumers; since the work takes a variable amount of time, the first consumer to finish takes the next URL off the list of events. This repeats until all work is done and the consumer issues demand for events once again.

This is a great improvement. Not only have we processed the pages faster, but we now have confidence that we can scale our pipeline when we need to. You can call scrape_pages/1 even when the consumers are still busy, so events will be queued up automatically. It is important to understand how this works, so we're going to briefly cover this next.

Buffering Events

At this point, you may suspect that producers keep dispatched events in memory—and you will be correct. Producers have a built-in buffer which is used whenever the number of dispatched events is greater than the total pending demand. As we saw earlier, events staying in the buffer are automatically granted to consumers who issue demand.

The default size of the buffer is 10,000 events for stages of type :producer, and :infinity for type :producer_consumer. However, both can be configured with a fixed capacity of our choice or :infinity. In the init/1 callback, we can provide the optional buffer_size parameter in the return tuple. Let's do a quick experiment and change the buffer_size to 1:

```
{:producer, initial_state, buffer_size: 1}
```

Then rerun the application. Call scrape_pages/1 with the same list of pages as before. The output this time will be different.

```
iex(1)> pages = ["google.com", "facebook.com",
  "apple.com", "netflix.com", "amazon.com"]

iex(2)> PageProducer.scrape_pages(pages)

[info]  PageConsumer received ["facebook.com"]
[info]  PageConsumer received ["google.com"]
[warn]  GenStage producer PageProducer has
  discarded 2 events from buffer
[info]  PageConsumer received ["amazon.com"]
[info]  PageProducer received demand for 1 pages
[info]  PageProducer received demand for 1 pages
```

We did this to demonstrate what happens when the buffer_size limit is exceeded. We received a warning, telling us how many events were dropped from the buffer and for which producer. Since demand by the two consumers was two events (one each), and we dispatched five events, we ended up with three extra events and no demand for them. Because buffer_size is 1, the first two events were dropped from the list. Only the last one was kept in the buffer and processed later.

Dropping Events from the End of the Buffer

 If you want to use a fixed-size buffer, you also have the option to discard events from the end of the queue when the :buffer_size limit is hit. Just pass the optional :buffer_keep param and set it to :first (the default value is :last).

Using the built-in buffer is convenient for most use cases. If you need fine-grain control over the number of events produced and dispatched, you may want to look into implementing your own queue for storing produced events and pending demand. Erlang's :queue[1] is a great option as it is already available in Elixir. Such a queue could be stored in producer's state, and used to dispatch events only when demand has been registered in handle_demand/3. This will also give you an opportunity to implement your custom logic for discarding events—useful if you want to prioritize one type of event over another.

Adding Concurrency with ConsumerSupervisor

Using multiple consumers to process events one by one, concurrently, is a very useful technique. To make this task even easier, GenStage comes with a special type of supervisor called ConsumerSupervisor. It works similarly to a consumer and can subscribe to one or more producers. It can also monitor, start, and restart child processes, just like a supervisor.

What makes ConsumerSupervisor special is that when it receives a list of events from a producer, it automatically starts a process for each event and passes the event as an argument to that process. When a child process exits successfully, new demand will be issued by ConsumerSupervisor and the cycle repeats. This figure illustrates how child processes are started on-demand when new events are received:

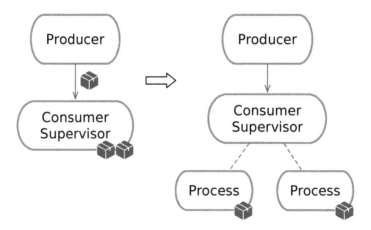

Next, we are going to refactor some of our existing logic using a ConsumerSupervisor to demonstrate how it works in practice.

Creating a ConsumerSupervisor

We're going to create a new file page_consumer_supervisor.ex and place it in the lib directory. Here are the full contents:

```
scraper/lib/page_consumer_supervisor.ex
defmodule PageConsumerSupervisor do
  use ConsumerSupervisor
  require Logger

  def start_link(_args) do
    ConsumerSupervisor.start_link(__MODULE__, :ok)
  end

  def init(:ok) do
    Logger.info("PageConsumerSupervisor init")

    children = [
      %{
        id: PageConsumer,
        start: {PageConsumer, :start_link, []},
        restart: :transient
      }
    ]

    opts = [
      strategy: :one_for_one,
      subscribe_to: [
        {PageProducer, max_demand: 2}
      ]
    ]

    ConsumerSupervisor.init(children, opts)
  end
end
```

This is a lot of new code, so let's break it down and explain how it works.

We named our module PageConsumerSupervisor and immediately after the defmodule declaration, we brought in the ConsumerSupervisor module logic. Since this is a process, we define the now familiar start_link/1 function. State is not relevant for ConsumerSupervisor, so we simply pass an :ok atom.

The init/1 function is more interesting. Here, we have to delegate the initialization to ConsumerSupervisor.init/2, which accepts two parameters, in this order:

- A list of child specifications. ConsumerSupervisor needs only one child spec, with a mandatory :restart key. The only restart options supported are :temporary and :transient.

- A list of arguments. Here you have to configure the subscription, using the :subscribe_to key, which works like the same option in the stages of type :consumer and :producer_consumer. We also set a supervisor strategy using the :strategy key, just like with a standard Supervisor process.

For the first parameter—the list of child specifications—we have created a children variable, which contains the specification to start the PageConsumer module. As we said already, we only need one child spec here. This is because ConsumerSupervisor will automatically replicate this child spec when starting new processes. You can think of it as a template, which will be used for all children processes.

We also have an opts variable holding the supervisor options. We picked the :one_for_one strategy, and we have also subscribed to PageProducer. Since PageConsumerSupervisor starts child processes for each event, min_demand and max_demand will tell the supervisor how many processes it needs to start, according to the demand. We are going to set max_demand to 2, which means that two consumers (at most) could run concurrently.

Hopefully these options are already familiar to you. If you have forgotten what they mean or have skipped some parts of the book, please refer to Chapter 2, Long-Running Processes Using GenServer, on page 25 for more information.

It may look like we have added a lot of new code, but with this setup, our consumer will become much simpler. Let's move on to that next.

The Simplified Consumer

As we mentioned before, PageConsumerSupervisor will wait for a child process to exit successfully, before it issues new demand. We know from Chapter 1, Easy Concurrency with the Task Module, on page 1 that the easiest way to start a new background process is to use the Task module. The Task.start_link/1 function can run our code in a process and then exit—exactly what we need. Here is our refactored PageConsumer:

```
scraper/lib/page_consumer.change3.ex
defmodule PageConsumer do
  require Logger

  def start_link(event) do
    Logger.info("PageConsumer received #{event}")

    Task.start_link(fn ->
      Scraper.work()
    end)
  end
end
```

PageConsumer is now just a few lines of code. This may be surprising and you probably wonder what happened with all other logic.

Remember that we told PageConsumerSupervisor to subscribe to PageProducer for events. This means that PageConsumerSupervisor has effectively taken the place of a :consumer in our data-processing pipeline. However, PageConsumerSupervisor only manages demand, receives events, and starts new processes. It doesn't do any work.

That's why we still need PageConsumer to process the events. Our event processing logic is still the same, but it has been moved from handle_events/3 to Task.start_link/1. Notice that we also no longer receive a list of one or more events, just a single event variable.

Although PageConsumer is no longer a GenStage of type :consumer, it is still a consumer of events, so we are going to stick to this convention and keep its name as it is.

Putting It All Together

Finally, we need to make a small change in our main application supervision tree in application.ex. We are going to remove the individual PageConsumer processes and add PageConsumerSupervisor in their place:

```
scraper/lib/scraper/application.change2.ex
children = [
  PageProducer,
➤  PageConsumerSupervisor
]
```

Let's rerun our application and call PageProducer.scrape_pages/1 in the IEx shell, using the same list of URLs:

```
iex(2)> PageProducer.scrape_pages(pages)

14:28:18.783 [info]  PageConsumer received google.com
14:28:18.785 [info]  PageConsumer received facebook.com
14:28:21.790 [info]  PageConsumer received apple.com
14:28:23.790 [info]  PageConsumer received netflix.com
14:28:25.791 [info]  PageConsumer received amazon.com
14:28:26.791 [info]  PageProducer received demand for 1 pages
14:28:27.792 [info]  PageProducer received demand for 1 pages
```

Great, everything works just like before, but we have significantly simplified our code. The supervisor will monitor processes and will restart them in case of an error. Furthermore, it is now even easier to scale our data-processing pipeline. We just have to go to PageConsumerSupervisor and increase max_demand.

How To Find Out the Number of Logical Cores at Runtime?

In Elixir, you can get the number of logical cores available programmatically by calling System.schedulers_online(). This could be useful if you want to set ConsumerSupervisor's max_demand dynamically, for example:

max_demand = System.schedulers_online() * 2

My personal laptop has a CPU with four logical cores, so max_demand will be eight using the formula above. However, when I deploy the application to a production server, it will run on a much more powerful machine with eight logical cores. As a result, the maximum number of concurrent processes will be sixteen—much better. For best results, always measure and adjust max_demand according to your use case.

It's worth highlighting that ConsumerSupervisor can start any kind of process. We picked Task.start_link/1 for simplicity and versatility. However, you can start GenServer processes or even GenStage producer processes if you need to. Keep in mind that all child processes must exit with reason :normal or :shutdown, so the supervisor can reissue demand. You can do this by returning {:stop, :normal, state} from a process callback when you're ready to terminate it. Most GenServer and GenStage callbacks support this return tuple, including handle_demand/3 and handle_events/3, which gives you a lot of flexibility.

Creating Multi-Stage Data Pipelines

We already demonstrated how :producer and :consumer stages work in practice. The only type of stage that we haven't seen in action yet is the :producer_consumer. Producer-consumer stages are the key to building infinitely complex data-processing pipelines. The good news is that if you understand how producers and consumers work, you already know producer-consumers.

When you learn how to add stages and extend your data pipelines, you may be tempted to start organizing your business logic using stages, rather than plain Elixir modules and functions. As the GenStage documentation warns us, this is an anti-pattern:

> If your domain has to process the data in multiple steps, you should write that logic in separate modules and not directly in a GenStage. You only add stages according to the runtime needs, typically when you need to provide back-pressure or leverage concurrency.

A good rule of thumb is to always start with plain functions. When you recognize the need for using back-pressure, create a two-stage data pipeline first.

As we are going to see in a moment, adding more stages is easy, so you can gradually extend it when you spot an opportunity for improvement.

Right, let's begin. First, we need to add some business logic that justifies adding another stage. Open scraper.ex and add the following function:

```
scraper/lib/scraper.change1.ex
def online?(_url) do
  # Pretend we are checking if the
  # service is online or not.
  work()

  # Select result randomly.
  Enum.random([false, true, true])
end
```

We are going to pretend that we are sending a network request to check if the website is online. Our work/1 function comes in handy, so we are going to use it to pause the current process. As the function name suggests, we return true or false, selected at random from three options: [false, true, true]. This way we have a 33% chance of the service being offline.

Now that our "business logic" is in place, let's add a new stage to our pipeline.

Adding a Producer-Consumer

We're going to name our new module OnlinePageProducerConsumer, so let's create online_page_producer_consumer.ex in the lib directory.

First, we're going to define the start_link/1 function:

```
scraper/lib/online_page_producer_consumer.ex
def start_link(_args) do
  initial_state = []
  GenStage.start_link(__MODULE__, initial_state, name: __MODULE__)
end
```

The start_link/1 function will take no arguments and have no state. It's important to set the :name key of the process so we can refer to it later. Next, add the init/1 function:

```
scraper/lib/online_page_producer_consumer.ex
def init(initial_state) do
  Logger.info("OnlinePageProducerConsumer init")

  subscription = [
    {PageProducer, min_demand: 0, max_demand: 1}
  ]

  {:producer_consumer, initial_state, subscribe_to: subscription}
end
```

The return tuple of our producer-consumer is very similar to the one we have in PageConsumer. However, notice that the type of stage is now :producer_consumer instead of :consumer.

Finally, we will implement the handle_events/3 callback:

```
scraper/lib/online_page_producer_consumer.ex
def handle_events(events, _from, state) do
  Logger.info("OnlinePageProducerConsumer received #{inspect(events)}")
  events = Enum.filter(events, &Scraper.online?/1)
  {:noreply, events, state}
end
```

To make things a bit more interesting, we are going to filter offline services and only dispatch URLs for websites that are online. That's correct—unlike :consumer stages, we can return a list of events from the handle_events/3 callback.

Producer-consumer stages can also implement handle_demand/3, just like any producer, but we will leave it out for now. It will dispatch no events by default.

The most difficult part is now over. All we have to do is plug the new stage into the pipeline.

Rewiring Our Pipeline

We want to scrape pages which are online, so PageConsumerSupervisor will no longer subscribe to PageProducer, but to OnlinePageProducerConsumer. Perhaps PageConsumerSupervisor and PageConsumer should be renamed to OnlinePageConsumerSupervisor and OnlinePageConsumer, respectively, but we'll leave them as they are for now.

Let's swap the following part in page_consumer_supervisor.ex:

```
scraper/lib/page_consumer_supervisor.ex
subscribe_to: [
  {PageProducer, max_demand: 2}
]
```

with

```
scraper/lib/page_consumer_supervisor.change1.ex
subscribe_to: [
  {OnlinePageProducerConsumer, max_demand: 2}
]
```

And edit application.ex to add the producer-consumer into the main supervision tree:

```
scraper/lib/scraper/application.change3.ex
children = [
  PageProducer,
```

```
➤    OnlinePageProducerConsumer,
     PageConsumerSupervisor
]
```

We added OnlinePageProducerConsumer before PageConsumerSupervisor on purpose. Producers always have to be started before the consumers. If we don't do that, the consumers won't be able to subscribe to them because the producer process would not be available.

That's it. We didn't have to change our external API, so you can start IEx and call PageProducer.scrape_pages/1 with our test list of pages. You should see something like this:

```
12:49:34.111 [info]  OnlinePageProducerConsumer received ["google.com"]
12:49:35.112 [info]  PageConsumer received google.com
12:49:35.112 [info]  OnlinePageProducerConsumer received ["facebook.com"]
12:49:36.113 [info]  PageConsumer received facebook.com
12:49:37.113 [info]  OnlinePageProducerConsumer received ["apple.com"]
12:49:38.114 [info]  OnlinePageProducerConsumer received ["netflix.com"]
12:49:41.115 [info]  OnlinePageProducerConsumer received ["amazon.com"]
12:49:45.116 [info]  PageProducer received demand for 1 pages
```

We have randomized our logic so the output will be slightly different every time. Nevertheless, the behavior will remain the same. We can see PageConsumer received only two events, and the rest were filtered out by OnlinePageProducerConsumer. We have successfully added another stage with minimal changes.

There is still room for improvement. We kept this example simple on purpose to show you how to extend your pipeline with additional stages. We used a single OnlinePageProducerConsumer process and limited its demand to only one event. In production, this could become a performance bottleneck.

To resolve this, we are going to leverage concurrency again by adding another OnlinePageProducerConsumer process to our supervision tree. This will increase our capacity and we will be able to check more pages at the same time.

Scaling Up a Stage with Extra Processes

Since we are adding more processes of the same type, let's create a Registry and start keeping track of them. We can add it as the first child process in our main supervision tree in application.ex:

```
children = [
  {Registry, keys: :unique, name: ProducerConsumerRegistry},
  PageProducer,
  OnlinePageProducerConsumer,
  PageConsumerSupervisor
]
```

If you want to refresh your memory on how to use Registry, please see Naming Processes Using the Registry, on page 49.

We called the new process ProducerConsumerRegistry to keep its name short, but you can also call it OnlinePageProducerConsumerRegistry if you'd like to be specific.

Next, we want to add another OnlinePageProducerConsumer, but we have to assign it a unique name and an id before adding it to the main supervision tree. We may want to add more of these processes in the future, so let's create a helper function to avoid repetitive code:

scraper/lib/scraper/application.change4.ex
```
def producer_consumer_spec(id: id) do
  id = "online_page_producer_consumer_#{id}"
  Supervisor.child_spec({OnlinePageProducerConsumer, id}, id: id)
end
```

The new producer_consumer_spec/1 helper accepts an id param, which we are going to prefix with the string online_page_producer_consumer_ for readability. Notice that the id is used as the unique process id when calling child_spec/2. It is also given to the process as an argument. You will see how we are going to use it in just a moment.

Now, let's use our helper function and see how it works:

scraper/lib/scraper/application.change4.ex
```
children = [
  {Registry, keys: :unique, name: ProducerConsumerRegistry},
  PageProducer,
  producer_consumer_spec(id: 1),
  producer_consumer_spec(id: 2),
  PageConsumerSupervisor
]
```

We used plain integers for the id param. Calling producer_consumer_spec(id: 1) will therefore return a process specification with an id online_page_producer_consumer_1. The same id is now available to us in the start_link/1 function for OnlinePageProducerConsumer:

scraper/lib/online_page_producer_consumer.change1.ex
```
def start_link(id) do
  initial_state = []
  GenStage.start_link(__MODULE__, initial_state, name: via(id))
end
```

Here's where the id comes in useful—we want to use the :via method of getting a process name and assign it to the process. This is all done in the via/1 helper function, which looks like so:

```
scraper/lib/online_page_producer_consumer.change1.ex
def via(id) do
  {:via, Registry, {ProducerConsumerRegistry, id}
end
```

We use the ProducerConsumerRegistry we created earlier to store a reference to our process.

We're almost there. The final piece of the puzzle is updating our PageConsumer-Supervisor—it needs to know which producers to subscribe to for events. The subscribe_to option for consumer stages is very flexible. We already know the short syntax that accepts a module name. You can also pass a process identifier, or use a :via tuple. We are going to use the latter, since we already have the via/1 helper defined in OnlinePageProducerConsumer:

```
scraper/lib/page_consumer_supervisor.change2.ex
subscribe_to: [
  {OnlinePageProducerConsumer.via("online_page_producer_consumer_1"), []},
  {OnlinePageProducerConsumer.via("online_page_producer_consumer_2"), []}
]
```

Now we have everything in place and we can give it a try by firing iex with the same test data:

```
iex(1)> PageProducer.scrape_pages(pages)

13:27:44.813 [info]  OnlinePageProducerConsumer received ["google.com"]
13:27:44.813 [info]  OnlinePageProducerConsumer received ["facebook.com"]
13:27:46.814 [info]  PageConsumer received facebook.com
13:27:47.815 [info]  OnlinePageProducerConsumer received ["apple.com"]
13:27:48.816 [info]  PageConsumer received apple.com
13:27:49.814 [info]  PageConsumer received google.com
13:27:51.815 [info]  OnlinePageProducerConsumer received ["amazon.com"]
13:27:51.817 [info]  OnlinePageProducerConsumer received ["netflix.com"]
13:27:52.816 [info]  PageConsumer received amazon.com
13:27:52.816 [info]  Received demand for 1 pages
13:27:52.818 [info]  Received demand for 1 pages
```

In the output above, we can see that both OnlinePageProducerConsumer processes picked up a website each. This helps us process an extra item while the other process is busy, so we effectively doubled our pipeline capacity for this stage of the pipeline with only a few changes. We can also extend this further by adding more OnlinePageProducerConsumer stages. The figure on page 84 illustrates what our final data-processing pipeline looks like.

Looking at the figure, you can appreciate the complexity of the system we have just built. Thanks to GenStage, we could focus on the business logic and overall architecture, so we didn't need to write lot of code, which is great.

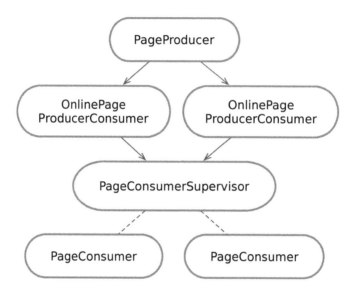

Hopefully this section helped you understand how :producer_consumer stages help us to build pipelines to tackle any problem. We covered a lot of material, but there is one more thing we're going to discuss before we wrap up.

Choosing the Right Dispatcher

There is one important component of GenStage we haven't talked about yet, and this component is the *dispatcher*. When :producer and :producer_consumer stages send events to consumers, it's in fact the dispatcher that takes care of sending the events. So far we have used the default DemandDispatcher, but GenStage comes with two more. Let's see what they do and how we can use them.

You can specify what dispatcher to use when initializing the process, using the :dispatcher key. The default is DemandDispatcher, which is equivalent to this configuration:

```
def init(state) do
  {:producer, state, dispatcher: GenStage.DemandDispatcher}
end
```

DemandDispatcher sends events to consumers with the highest demand first. It is the dispatcher that you're going to use most often. However, there are cases where you may want to route events to consumers using a different strategy, and this is where BroadcastDispatcher and PartitionDispatcher come in. Let's look at BroadcastDispatcher first.

Using BroadcastDispatcher

You can switch to BroadcastDispatcher by setting :dispatcher to GenStage.BroadcastDispatcher in your init/1 function:

```
{:producer, state, dispatcher: GenStage.BroadcastDispatcher}
```

As its name suggests, BroadcastDispatcher sends the events supplied by the :producer or :producer_consumer to *all* consumers subscribed to it. This is useful when you have different types of consumers subscribed to the same producer, and need the same data, but for different purposes.

When BroadcastDispatcher is used, consumer stages get the ability to filter the events they are receiving. This means that each consumer can opt-in for specific events, and discard the rest. All you have to do is use the :selector setting when subscribing to the producer, like so:

```
def init(state) do
  selector =
    fn incoming_event ->
      # you can use the event to decide whether
      # to return `true` and accept it, or `false` to reject it.
    end
  sub_opts = [
    {SomeProducer, selector: selector}
  ]
  {:consumer, state, subscribe_to: sub_opts}
end
```

As you can see, the :selector is just a function, which you can optionally pass to each producer individually. The consumer is the one that has to examine each message, and decide whether it wants it or not.

The other type of dispatcher we're going to look at also helps you route events to specific consumers, but it works in a slightly different way.

Using PartitionDispatcher

Unlike BroadcastDispatcher, where the consumer has to check each event, PartitionDispatcher leaves this responsibility to the producer. The producer examines each event, and assigns it to a *partition*. You can think of partitions as buckets, which we use to put one or more events in. Consumers can then tell the producer what type of events they want to receive, based on that partition.

There are two extra arguments that we need to pass when configuring PartitionDispatcher—:partitions and :hash. Here is an example:

```
def init(state) do
  hash =
    fn event ->
      # you can use the event to decide which partition
      # to assign it to, or use `:none` to ignore it.
      {event, :c}
    end

  opts = [
    partitions: [:a, :b, :c],
    hash: hash
  ]

  {:producer, state, dispatcher: {GenStage.ParitionDispatcher, opts}}
end
```

The hash function is similar to the selector function in BroadcastDispatcher, but it has to return a tuple, rather than a boolean. The tuple should contain the event that we want to dispatch, and the name of the partition. Partitions are chosen by us and could be any Elixir term. Here we picked :a, :b, and :c. You can also ignore an event by passing :none, which you don't have to define in your :partitions list. Also notice that the :dispatcher value is now a tuple, which allows us to pass the dispatcher configuration options as the second element in the tuple.

Now that the producer is configured, consumers can subscribe to one of the partitions when initializing:

```
sub_opts = [
  {SomeProducer, partition: :b}
]

{:consumer, state, subscribe_to: sub_opts}
```

BroadcastDispatcher and PartitionDispatcher are a great addition to the default DemandDispatcher, and should help you adapt your data-processing pipeline to an ever-wider variety of uses cases.

However, if they still don't quite match what you are trying to accomplish, you can also create your own dispatcher from scratch, by implementing the GenStage.Dispatcher behaviour. Check out the Dispatcher module documentation[2] for more information on what callbacks you have to implement.

Now it's time for a quick recap.

---

2.   https://hexdocs.pm/gen_stage/GenStage.Dispatcher.html#content

Wrapping Up

This chapter wasn't the easiest, so congratulations on completing it! Although slightly intimidating at first, GenStage is a brilliant tool that makes other programming languages jealous of Elixir. Of course, as José Valim has pointed out many times, none of it would be possible without Erlang's rock-solid OTP serving as a foundation.

In this chapter, we looked at back-pressure and the problems it solves when building and scaling data-processing pipelines. You learned about GenStage and how stages enable us to use back-pressure to easily build data-processing pipelines. We saw how you can scale your system to handle increased workloads by leveraging concurrency with ConsumerSupervisor. When working on more complex tasks, multi-stage pipelines can help model and tackle potential challenges. You can use and adapt these techniques to build resilient and scalable systems that perform well under increased workloads.

> ### Further reading
>
> You saw that GenStage is very versatile and can be configured in many different ways to solve an endless variety of problems. Although we covered a lot of ground, we have only seen a fraction of what's possible. There are more advanced features in GenStage that didn't make it in this chapter, such as the ability to switch to :manual subscription mode in stages of type :consumer and :producer_consumer. This gives you the flexibility to change demand at runtime, rather than hard-coding max_demand and min_demand at compile time.
>
> These and other features are well documented online, so I would encourage you to check GenStage's official documentation[a] and explore further what's available.
>
> ---
>
> a.   https://hexdocs.pm/gen_stage/GenStage.html

Working with GenStage could be challenging. In order for your data-processing pipeline to work, everything has to be configured and set up correctly. To achieve the desired level of concurrency, you may have to create more than a few types of stages. Often this makes GenStage a less appealing choice for more common tasks and problems, especially in teams less experienced with it. The good news is José and team have worked on two more libraries—Flow and Broadway—which are built on top of GenStage and are designed to solve specific problems with less configuration and set up. In the next chapter, we're going to learn about Flow, which provides a high-level API for working with collections of data, similar to the Enum and Stream modules. We're going to cover Broadway straight after that in the final chapter.

CHAPTER 4

Processing Collections with Flow

Since Elixir is a functional language and all data is immutable, most Elixir developers quickly get accustomed to using functions like map, filter, and reduce on a daily basis. These and other data-processing functions, found in the Enum and Stream modules, are essential to functional programming and help us transform data in a variety of ways.

However, as the amount of data that you have to process grows, so does the time it takes to finish the work. You already have a few tools at your disposal that you can use to run code concurrently, but implementing frequently used functions like reduce and group_by in parallel is going to be challenging. Thankfully, there is already a solution that's available to us on the Hex registry.

In this chapter, you're going to learn about Flow—a powerful library with a simple API that makes processing large collections of data a breeze. Flow uses GenStage under the hood, so all operations will run in parallel in separate stage processes, taking care of back-pressure for you.

First, we are going to introduce Flow, comparing it to the commonly used Enum and Stream modules, by analyzing airport data from around the world. You will see how easy it is to convert existing code to run concurrently and work with large datasets. Then we'll look at how to run reduce operations concurrently and handle infinite and slow streams of data. Finally, we will revisit the scraper project and integrate Flow with an already running GenStage pipeline, which will give you some extra flexibility when solving problems. Let's get started!

Analyzing Airports Data

Before we begin, let's scaffold a new project to work on. We are going to build a simple utility to help us analyze airport data by country. We will see which countries and territories have the biggest number of working airports in the world. Let's call this application airports:

```
$ mix new airports
```

Next, let's edit mix.exs to add flow as a dependency. We are also going to need a CSV parser. Change your dependencies list to this:

airports/mix.exs
```
defp deps do
  [
    {:flow, "~> 1.0"},
    {:nimble_csv, "~> 1.1"}
  ]
end
```

Once you're done, run mix deps.get to download the dependencies.

We also have to download the dataset itself. The one we are going to use has been published by OurAirports and is available to download here.[1]

Find the link, and download the file airports.csv. We pick this file for convenience, since it is only about 9 MB in size, so it is easy to download. However, you can use exactly the same set of tools and techniques even when working with large datasets that are gigabytes in size. The file contains a lot of interesting information about airports from around the world:

- id and official name of each airport
- latitude_deg and longitude_deg with the exact coordinates
- iso_country of the country where the airport is based, such as US or JP
- type which could be one of several values, including heliport, seaplane_base, or closed

Feel free to have a look at the contents of the file to get a better sense of what's in the dataset.

Next, within the airports project folder, create a folder called priv. Copy and paste the airports.csv file there. Your project file structure should end up looking similar to this:

```
.
├── lib
│   └── airports.ex
├── mix.exs
├── mix.lock
└── priv
    └── airports.csv
```

---

1.   https://ourairports.com/data

Let's add a function to help us retrieve the path to the file. Edit airports.ex and replace the contents of the Airports module with this function:

```
airports/lib/airports.ex
def airports_csv() do
  Application.app_dir(:airports, "/priv/airports.csv")
end
```

The Application.app_dir/1 helper returns the full path to the :airports application, while the second argument in app_dir/2 appends the path within that application folder and returns it. This means that we will have the correct path to the CSV file, regardless of the file system or build environment used. We will use this function later on to read the file from the file system.

Finally, we opted for nimble_csv, a highly efficient and very configurable parser. It has a built-in module NimbleCSV.RFC4180, which parses the common RFC4180 file format. We are going to alias this module to CSV. This is optional, but it helps keep the examples in this book shorter:

```
airports/lib/airports.ex
defmodule Airports do
  alias NimbleCSV.RFC4180, as: CSV
```

Now we're ready to start writing some code!

Creating Flows and Reading Files

Reading files from the file system is easy with Elixir, but there are a few things you have to consider when consuming file data and transforming it to common Elixir data structures. In this section, we will introduce Flow by comparing it to the Enum and Stream modules and see how we can reduce system memory usage and increase performance when reading files.

We are going to add a function that returns all airports from the airports.csv file that are currently in operation. To do this, we have to read the file and remove all closed airports from the list of results. We will convert the results to an Elixir Map, keeping only the data attributes that we are interested in.

We will start with the most obvious implementation. Add the following function to the Airports module:

```
airports/lib/airports.ex
def open_airports() do
  airports_csv()
  |> File.read!()
  |> CSV.parse_string()
  |> Enum.map(fn row ->
    %{
```

```
      id: Enum.at(row, 0),
      type: Enum.at(row, 2),
      name: Enum.at(row, 3),
      country: Enum.at(row, 8)
    }
  end)
  |> Enum.reject(&(&1.type == "closed"))
end
```

Let's break down this function to understand what it does.

First, we use the airports_csv/0 helper to get the path to the CSV file, and call File.read!/1 with the result. This will read the file, and the contents will be passed onto the CSV.parse_string/1 function. Here, CSV is the parser module from the NimbleCSV library. The result of parsing the file will be a list of rows, and each row is also represented as a list of values.

Having each row as a list is not very convenient. Using Enum.map/2, we convert each item from a list to a map, using descriptive keys for each value. We will just concentrate on four fields to keep things simple: id, type, name, and country. The rest are discarded.

Now that we have a nicer data structure to work with, we can use Enum.reject/2 to check if an airport's type value is closed and remove closed ones from the list.

Let's see if this function works as promised. Start an IEx session by running iex -S mix in your terminal, and run Airports.open_airports():

```
iex(1)> Airports.open_airports()
[
  %{
    country: "US",
    id: "323361",
    name: "Aero B Ranch Airport",
    type: "small_airport"
  },
  %{
    country: "US",
    id: "6527",
    name: "Cordes Airport",
    type: "small_airport"
  },
  ...
```

Notice that the output contains only non-closed type of airports, which means that our function works correctly.

However, there are issues with this approach, which would cause problems when you work with larger files. The biggest one is using File.read!/1 to read the entire file and keep it in memory, so CSV.parse_string/1 can parse it. A large file will quickly eat up your system memory, potentially bringing the whole application to a halt. We also iterate over each item in the list twice, using map/2 and filter/2, building two lists as we go. We can take a quick measurement of how long the function takes to complete, using Erlang's :timer.tc/1 helper. Run this in your IEx shell:

```
iex(2)> :timer.tc(&Airports.open_airports/0)
{2959203,
 [
   %{country: "US", id: "6523", name: "Total Rf Heliport", type: "heliport"},
 ...
```

The :timer.tc/1 function returns a tuple. The first value is the actual function duration in microseconds; the second is the result. From this output, we can see that open_airports/0 took about 3000ms to complete on my machine. Let's see how we can improve this.

Benchmarking Functions

 In this chapter we are using :timer.tc/1 to measure how long the function takes to run. This is just for convenience and to keep the examples short. If you want to benchmark performance, it is best to use a benchmarking library, such as benchee.[2]

Improving Performance with Streams

We already discussed streams and the Stream module in Managing Series of Tasks, on page 11. You know that the Stream data structure is lazily evaluated, allowing you to process data only when it's needed. The Stream module has lazy implementations of map/2, filter/2, and other functions. We can use Stream.map/2 and Stream.filter/2 to replace their Enum counterparts, but what about reading and parsing the file?

Don't worry, Elixir has you covered. The File module has a lazy equivalent to read!/1 called stream!/1, which is exactly what we need. Finally, the CSV module has parse_stream/1, which you can use to replace parse_string/1. We have everything we need to convert our code from eager to lazy. Here is the new version:

airports/lib/airports.change1.ex
```
def open_airports() do
  airports_csv()
  |> File.stream!()
  |> CSV.parse_stream()
```

---

2. https://hex.pm/packages/benchee

```
  |> Stream.map(fn row ->
    %{
      id: :binary.copy(Enum.at(row, 0)),
      type: :binary.copy(Enum.at(row, 2)),
      name: :binary.copy(Enum.at(row, 3)),
      country: :binary.copy(Enum.at(row, 8))
    }
  end)
  |> Stream.reject(&(&1.type == "closed"))
  |> Enum.to_list()
end
```

You can see that the code looks mostly the same. One notable difference is that we are using :binary.copy/1 inside Stream.map/2, which is needed to copy the data from parse_stream/1. This is documented online[3] if you'd like to read more.

Let's run recompile() in IEx and check if this version indeed performs better:

```
iex(3)> :timer.tc(&Airports.open_airports/0)
{590915,
 [
   %{country: "US", id: "6523", name: "Total Rf Heliport", type: "heliport"},
 ...
```

The function now took almost 600ms. We achieved five times better performance with just a few small changes.

But, we can do even better. All code so far is running synchronously in the current process. The good news is that we can make our code run concurrently with very small changes, using Flow.

Working with JSON Files

 Unlike the CSV format, JSON is a lot more complicated to parse. At the time of writing, the most popular JSON parsers for Elixir, Jason and Poison, do not support streaming. If you are working with large JSON files, check out Erlang's jsx[4] or Elixir's Jaxon.[5]

Running Streams Concurrently

To use Flow, we need to convert an existing data source first. The result of the conversion is called a *flow*. Using Flow.from_enumerable/2, we can create a flow from a stream. We are going to discuss how from_enumerable/2 works in a moment.

---

3.   https://hexdocs.pm/nimble_csv/NimbleCSV.html#module-binary-references
4.   https://hex.pm/packages/jsx
5.   https://hex.pm/packages/jaxon

Let's change open_airports/0 once again. This time we are going to replace Stream.map/2 and Stream.reject/2 with Flow.map/2 and Flow.reject/2. Make sure to measure the performance afterwards. Here is how the code looks after the changes:

```
airports/lib/airports.change2.ex
def open_airports() do
  airports_csv()
  |> File.stream!()
  |> CSV.parse_stream()
  |> Flow.from_enumerable()
  |> Flow.map(fn row ->
    %{
      id: :binary.copy(Enum.at(row, 0)),
      type: :binary.copy(Enum.at(row, 2)),
      name: :binary.copy(Enum.at(row, 3)),
      country: :binary.copy(Enum.at(row, 8))
    }
  end)
  |> Flow.reject(&(&1.type == "closed"))
  |> Enum.to_list()
end
```

However, this version took about 1300ms. It is still faster than our original implementation, but it is twice as slow as the previous one. Something has gone wrong.

Looking closer at the code, it looks like we have created a bottleneck. The flow is based on a single data source—the result of the parse_stream/1 function—which might have trouble keeping up. Let's move the parsing logic into the Flow.map/2 function, so it runs concurrently with the rest of the code:

```
airports/lib/airports.change2.ex
def open_airports() do
  airports_csv()
  |> File.stream!()
  |> Flow.from_enumerable()
  |> Flow.map(fn row ->
    [row] = CSV.parse_string(row, skip_headers: false)

    %{
      id: Enum.at(row, 0),
      type: Enum.at(row, 2),
      name: Enum.at(row, 3),
      country: Enum.at(row, 8)
    }
  end)
  |> Flow.reject(&(&1.type == "closed"))
  |> Enum.to_list()
end
```

Running this version will give you much better results on a multi-core machine. On my machine, the function takes only about 300ms. Notice that we no longer need to use parse_stream/1 or :binary.copy/1, since we reverted to parsing with parse_string/1. Another small change is that when using parse_string/1, we had to set the :skip_headers option to false, which is required when the CSV string has no headers included. We need this because we parse each row individually, rather than the whole file.

We used from_enumerable/2 to create a flow, so you may wonder what the function actually does. Let's look at how flows work next.

Understanding Flows

Under the hood, a flow is a simple %Flow{} struct. It's a data structure that keeps track of the operations we want to perform, similar to how Elixir streams keep track of the functions to run.

However, unlike streams, flow operations run in GenStage stage processes, making them concurrent. When we used from_enumerable/2, Flow would treat the data source as a producer, where each element is sent down the flow as a GenStage event. Operations like Flow.map/2 and Flow.filter/2 will act as :consumer or :producer_consumer stages. All stage processes will start on demand, and stop when the data is fully processed. Without knowing it, we were using a data-processing pipeline to process the data.

Flow lets you configure the stage processes by passing a list of options as the second argument in from_enumerable/2. As you know, the number of stage processes determines the level of concurrency. By default, Flow uses the value of System.schedulers_online/0. This is usually the total number of virtual cores your machine has. You can change this by passing the :stages option and giving it an integer as the value. You can also tweak the demand by passing :max_demand and :min_demand, just like we did with GenStage.

Other than using from_enumerable/2, you can also use from_enumerables/2 to create a flow. It works in the same way, but accepts a list of enumerables, rather than a single one. This is useful when you work with multiple data sources. Later in this chapter, we will also see how to create a flow from existing GenStage stages, allowing you to plug Flow into an existing data-processing pipeline.

When it comes to data sources, any data structure that implements the Enumerable protocol can be consumed to start a flow. However, when working with large volumes of finite data, it's best to opt for libraries that use streams. So far, we saw examples with File.Stream and NimbleCSV, but other popular tools in the ecosystem support streaming as well. For example, Ecto provides Repo.stream/1 to stream results from database queries, and HTTP libraries like finch[6] also support streaming the results of an HTTP request.

Of course, we have only scratched the surface of what Flow can do. In the next section, we are going to cover reducing, grouping, and sorting data in parallel, and much more. Keep reading.

Working with Very Large Files

 When working with very large files, reading from the file system itself can become a bottleneck, too. In these cases, consider splitting the file into multiple chunks, using a command-line utility such as split. You can then use File.stream!/1 for each file, and Flow.from_enumerables/2 to consume all independent streams concurrently. You can also pass the :read_ahead option to File.stream!/1 to increase the number of lines read at a time.

Performing Reduce Concurrently with Partitions

In addition to map and filter, the reduce function in the Enum module is another frequently used tool when working with data. It is also the backbone of other functions in this module, including group_by, uniq_by, and take_sort. In this section, you will see how to use Flow.reduce/3 to count the number of working airports in each country present in the dataset in parallel. Then we'll move on to other convenience functions for grouping and sorting data. But before we begin, it is useful to understand how reduce works in Flow.

In reduce we have something called an accumulator, which could be any data type, and holds the latest state. Each element in the list we want to process is given to a *reducer* function, followed by the accumulator value, which is often shortened to acc for brevity. Once all items in the list have been transformed using the reducer function, the last accumulator value becomes the result of the reduce operation. Here is the blueprint of Enum.reduce/2:

```
Enum.reduce(enumerable, fn item, acc ->
  # Inside the reducer function you can
  # use the `item` event, and
  # return the `acc` value.
  acc
end)
```

Just like with Flow.map/2, each reducer function will run concurrently by default. However, if you directly replace Enum.reduce/2 with Flow.reduce/3 in your own code, you will see unexpected results. Since each reducer function runs in its own

---

6. https://hex.pm/packages/finch

process, it has no knowledge of other accumulator values. The final outcome will be the combined list of all results, which will contain duplicates. Let's demonstrate the issue by adding Flow.reduce/3 to open_airports/0, just before Enum.to_list/1:

```
# ...
|> Flow.reject(&(&1.type == "closed"))
|> Flow.reduce(fn -> %{} end, fn item, acc ->
  Map.update(acc, item.country, 1, &(&1 + 1))
end)
|> Enum.to_list()
```

Notice that we're setting the starting value of the accumulator to %{} (an empty map), by passing a function that returns the initial value. Now, when you recompile and run the code, you should see something similar to this:

```
iex(4)> Airports.open_airports()
[
  {"AU", 2},
  {"BR", 321},
  {"CA", 464},
  {"CD", 23},
  {"CR", 2},
  {"EC", 86},
  {"FK", 1},
  {"GB", 1},
  ...
```

The list contains many items, so the result is most likely trimmed in IEx and you won't see the full output. You can use IO.inspect/2 with the :limit option set to :infinity to see everything:

```
iex(4)> Airports.open_airports() |> IO.inspect(limit: :infinity)
```

When inspecting the result on your machine, notice that many country codes appear more than once. This is the issue we wanted to demonstrate. With Enum.reduce/3, each country result will appear just once, but this is not the case here. Let's see why this happens and how to fix the results.

Routing Events with Partitions

As we know, Enum.reduce/3 works within a single process. With Flow.reduce/3, we have many processes, where each one continuously receives batches of items to work on. This is so Flow can balance the workload and handle back-pressure. However, items that should be counted together can end up being consumed by more than one process, so we get duplicates when all results are combined together in the end. The figure on page 99 illustrates the problem.

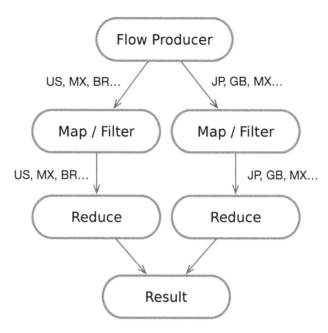

We can verify this by doing a quick experiment: let's use the :stages option to reduce concurrency to 1 when we call Flow.from_enumerable/1, like so:

```
|> Flow.from_enumerable(stages: 1)
```

If you recompile and rerun the function, you'll see that the result is now correct. However, this is not really a viable fix, because we lost the power of concurrency. Let's remove the stages: 1 argument.

The real solution to our problem is *partitioning*. Flow provides a function called partition/2, which creates another layer of stages that act like a router. You can specify a :key for each item going through the partition. When a key is computed, Flow will guarantee that same-key items will be sent to the same reducer process, as shown in the figure on page 100.

If this sounds familiar, this is because partition/2 uses GenStage.PartitionDispatcher under the hood, which we discussed in Choosing the Right Dispatcher, on page 84.

The :key option accepts three types of values:

- {:elem, position} for tuples, where position is an integer, so you can specify which element in the tuple to use as the key

- {:key, key} for maps, where key is a top-level key, and could be either an atom or a string

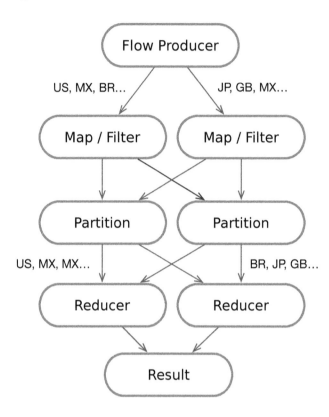

- An anonymous function returning a key, for more complex cases, like nested maps or computing the key based on several values. The function receives the item as an argument, for example, fn item -> .. end.

In our open_airports/0 logic, we count items by the :country attribute. Let's add a partition layer that ensures that items sharing the same :country value are sent to the same reducer:

```
airports/lib/airports.change3.ex
|> Flow.reject(&(&1.type == "closed"))
|> Flow.partition(key: {:key, :country})
|> Flow.reduce(fn -> %{} end, fn item, acc ->
  Map.update(acc, item.country, 1, &(&1 + 1))
end)
|> Enum.to_list()
```

You will now get the results we expected from the reduce function, and there will be no more duplicates.

Right now, the reduce function is effectively grouping results by country code and counting the number of airports at the same time. In the next section,

you will see an alternative way of doing this that might yield better performance in some use cases. We will also show how to sort the results, and find
out which are the top ten countries in the world with the most airports.

Grouping and Sorting

Just like Enum.group_by/2, Flow.group_by/2 groups the data by the given criteria.
They are also both implemented using reduce behind the scenes. Therefore,
we're going to keep our Flow.partition/2 function to continue routing events to
the correct process. This will ensure that airports of the same country are
grouped by the same process.

Let's replace Flow.reduce/3 with Flow.group_by/2:

```
airports/lib/airports.change3.ex
|> Flow.reject(&(&1.type == "closed"))
|> Flow.partition(key: {:key, :country})
|> Flow.group_by(& &1.country)
|> Flow.map(fn {country, data} -> {country, Enum.count(data)} end)
|> Enum.to_list()
```

The result of group_by/2 is a list of tuples, where the first element is the group
key, and the second is the group items. We added Flow.map/2 to transform this
output, replacing the group items element with a counter.

Rerunning the function in IEx should produce a result similar to what we've
seen before:

```
[
  {"BW", 120},
  {"CA", 2141},
  {"DO", 34},
  {"HK", 6},
  {"IO", 1},
  {"KP", 91},
  {"LY", 60},
  {"MA", 34},
  {"SY", 27},
  {"AR", 828},
  ...
]
```

Using Flow.group_by/2 is more convenient than Flow.reduce/3 if your only goal is to
group the elements in the list. Depending on your use case, you may also
benefit slightly from grouping the items first, before doing something else
with the grouped data, as we've done here. As always, benchmark your code
to find the best approach.

Now, let's make one final change to our logic: we will display only the top ten countries, ordered by the number of airports.

So far, we have seen that most functions in the Enum module have a direct equivalent in Flow. However, sorting is one of the exceptions. Normally, you would use Enum.sort/2 followed by Enum.take/2. Flow has take_sort/3, which combines the two functions into one. It works concurrently across all reducer stages, by performing the sort function and taking the specified number of items from each stage. Finally, it combines the output from all stages into a single result, by performing the same process one last time. Let's see it in action:

```
airports/lib/airports.change3.ex
|> Flow.reject(&(&1.type == "closed"))
|> Flow.partition(key: {:key, :country})
|> Flow.group_by(& &1.country)
|> Flow.map(fn {country, data} -> {country, Enum.count(data)} end)
|> Flow.take_sort(10, fn {_, a}, {_, b} -> a > b end)
|> Enum.to_list()
|> List.flatten()
```

This is the final result after sorting:

```
[
  {"US", 21406},
  {"BR", 4995},
  {"CA", 2141},
  {"AU", 1990},
  {"MX", 1372},
  {"KR", 1343},
  {"GB", 1004},
  {"RU", 938},
  {"DE", 888},
  {"FR", 830}
]
```

Note that we are also calling List.flatten/1 in the end. This is because the final result of Enum.to_list() contains a single nested list—the ordered items returned by take_sort/3. Calling flatten/1 will squash the results to eliminate the nesting, so the result is easier to work with.

We can see that the country with the biggest number of airports in the world is the United States, followed by Brazil and Canada. We use the broader definition of an airport and include helicopter pads as well as sea plane bases when counting, in addition to airports serving commercial flights. You can try to narrow the results, and experiment with Flow using the dataset to get more interesting insights.

While working with finite, bounded data is very common, there are cases where you have to deal with unbounded streams data. Flow has been designed to work with infinite data from the beginning. In the next section, you will learn about two important concepts in Flow—*windows* and *triggers*.

Running a Flow

Similar to streams, we've been using Enum.to_list/0 at the end of our flow pipelines, which forces them to run and produce a result. However, if you're not interested in the final result, you can use Flow.run/1 instead of Enum.to_list/0. It works similar to Stream.run/1 and always returns :ok.

Using Windows and Triggers

Operations like Flow.reduce/3, group_by/2, and take_sort/3 require all events to complete before producing a result. After all, you cannot group or sort a list without having all the data in the list available to you. But what if the data source keeps producing events for a really long time, or keeps producing events forever? This means that you will have to wait for a result either a very long time, or indefinitely. To avoid this, Flow introduces *windows* and *triggers*. In this section, you will see how they can help you get progress updates with long-running flows.

All events going through Flow are grouped together by a window. You can think of windows as folders for events—they allow you to organize the data in a way that's convenient for you. So far, we've been using Flow.Window.global/0, which creates a *global* window for us by default. Global windows group all events together and close only when all events have been received. These are other types of windows:

- Flow.Window.fixed/3 groups events by a timestamp value on the event, using specified time duration.

- Flow.Window.periodic/2 is like fixed/3 but groups events by processing time.

- Flow.Window.count/1 groups events when they reach the given count.

Windows also influence how reducer operations work. At the beginning of a window, the accumulator is reset, so it can start collecting data again from scratch. Remember that Flow.reduce/3 uses a function to create the initial accumulator value. This function is called at the beginning of each window.

You can also specify a *trigger* for each window. Triggers work like checkpoints and all trigger functions take a window as their first argument. When a trigger event occurs, you have the opportunity to take data out of the flow by specifying what events to emit. You can even change the accumulator value on-the-fly. These are available triggers:

- Flow.Window.trigger_every/2 triggers when you reach the given count of events.
- Flow.Window.trigger_periodically/3 triggers at the specified time duration.
- Flow.Window.trigger/3 is used for implementing custom triggers.

By default, every flow has an internal trigger for an event called :done, which occurs when there is no data left to process.

Depending on the type of window and trigger you choose, you can get different insights into the flow. In a moment, you'll see how to use trigger_every/2 with the default global window. We are not going to cover all possible combinations in this book, but the good news is that they are well documented online, and you can use them in a similar way. I encourage you to check out the official documentation for the Flow.Window module[7] after you complete this chapter.

We've covered the basics of windows and triggers, but there is one important thing left—detecting when a trigger occurs. Luckily, there is a function that makes this very easy.

Catching Trigger Events with on_trigger/2

We are going to use Flow.on_trigger/2 to run some code whenever a trigger occurs. This function gives you a lot of information about the state of the flow, so let's break it down and explain how it works.

Flow.on_trigger/2 takes an existing flow as its first argument and a callback function as its second. This callback function can take one, two, or three arguments, so you can choose the function arity that works best for your use case. These three arguments are available:

- The latest accumulator from the reducer

- Partition information as a tuple, containing the current partition index, and total number of partitions in use

- Window information as a tuple, containing the window name, window identifier, and trigger information

The trigger information is particularly useful. This value could be just the :done atom, when the data we are processing is not infinite. It could be a tuple,

---

7.   https://hexdocs.pm/flow/Flow.Window.html

containing the trigger type and configuration, for example, {:every, 500} or {:periodically, 5, :minute}.

Having all this information available to us is great, because it allows us to customize the behavior of the callback function, based on the state of the flow.

Finally, the return value for on_trigger/2 must be a tuple, where the first element is a list of events. This list of events is what the trigger will emit and send down the flow. The second element is the new accumulator value.

Now that you know how on_trigger/2 works, let's put everything together by making some changes to the airports project.

Getting Snapshots from Slow-Running or Infinite Flows

So far we've been using a CSV file as our main data source, which Elixir processes immediately. In order to demonstrate how windows and triggers work, we are going to intentionally slow down the file stream events by using Process.sleep/1. We'll also modify our business logic. We'll still group all data by country code, but this time we are going to capture progress snapshots every one thousand events. Let's start by slowing the stream of events:

airports/lib/airports.change4.ex
```
airports_csv()
|> File.stream!()
|> Stream.map(fn event ->
  Process.sleep(Enum.random([0, 0, 0, 1]))
  event
end)
|> Flow.from_enumerable()
```

Since we have tens of thousands of rows in our CSV file, we will randomly delay some of the events for one millisecond only. The rest of the events will go through without a delay. This means that the flow will still complete (eventually), but it won't be as quick as before.

You can try running this version of the code; it should take about a minute to complete.

Next, define the window variable at the top of the function like so:

airports/lib/airports.change4.ex
```
window = Flow.Window.trigger_every(Flow.Window.global(), 1000)
```

Now you can give it as an argument to Flow.partition/2:

airports/lib/airports.change4.ex
```
|> Flow.partition(window: window, key: {:key, :country})
```

Finally, let's add the trigger logic:

```
airports/lib/airports.change4.ex
|> Flow.group_by(& &1.country)
|> Flow.on_trigger(fn acc, _partition_info, {_type, _id, trigger} ->
  # Show progress in IEx, or use the data for something else.
  events =
    acc
    |> Enum.map(fn {country, data} -> {country, Enum.count(data)} end)
    |> IO.inspect(label: inspect(self()))

  case trigger do
    :done ->
      {events, acc}

    {:every, 1000} ->
      {[], acc}
  end
end)
|> Enum.to_list()
```

We are using the ternary callback function with on_trigger/2 so we can access all three arguments. Within the callback function, you have the opportunity to use the snapshot data in whichever way you want. For example, you can update your database to persist the events or send them elsewhere for processing. We chose to use IO.inspect/2 and print the events list containing the country code and number of airports. This way we can see some progress in IEx as the processes do their work. Notice that we're using the :label argument with IO.inspect/2 to print the PID of the reducer process—you'll see why we're doing this in a second.

We used pattern-matching to handle the :done trigger separately from the {:every, 1000} trigger. The latter occurs because we configured the window using Flow.Window.trigger_every/2 with a value of 1000. When the :done trigger happens, we emit the final result as a list of tuples. In case of {:every, 1000}, we do not emit anything, since we're not finished processing yet.

Let's run this in IEx. Results will start printing in your terminal as data is processed by Flow, and they should look similar to this:

```
...
#PID<0.431.0>: [{"MP", 1}, {"US", 6999}]
#PID<0.431.0>: [{"CN", 1}, {"MP", 1}, {"US", 7998}]
#PID<0.433.0>: [{"BF", 2}, {"BR", 992}, {"CH", 6}]
#PID<0.425.0>: [{"BW", 53}, {"CA", 947}]
#PID<0.431.0>: [{"MP", 1}, {"US", 8996}, {"XK", 2}]
#PID<0.428.0>: [{"CZ", 162}, {"DE", 506}, {"PG", 302}]
...
```

We know that Flow processes all data in parallel, and thanks to partitioning, each reducer stage process is guaranteed to have its own unique set of results. You can easily see this by comparing the debug output and process identifiers.

Let's make this change to the partition/2 function:

```
|> Flow.partition(stages: 1, window: window, key: {:key, :country})
```

Setting the :stages key to 1 will limit the concurrency to just one reducer process. This also makes the :key argument redundant, since there is only one stage to route events to, but we will leave it for now.

Let's restart IEx and run the function again. You will see the same PID in debug output, which means that a single reducer process will hold all the data.

Limiting concurrency like this is useful in some cases, for example, when debugging or when you need all accumulated data in one place. For now, let's revert the previous change by removing stages: 1 from partition/2.

When you run open_airports/0 and wait for a bit, eventually the function will complete. The final output will look similar to this:

```
[
  {"AM", 9},
  {"AO", 94},
  {"BH", 5},
  {"ES", 423},
  {"FJ", 30},
  {"JE", 1},
  {"LV", 59},
  {"ML", 31},
  ...
```

The final result contains all events emitted by on_trigger/2, in the order they were sent down the flow. We can use Flow.departition/5, which merges all existing stages into one using the provided merger function. In this particular case, the number of events in the result is small enough to be easily processed using the Enum module. If you want to return only the top ten countries, you can replace Enum.to_list() with this:

```
|> Enum.sort(fn {_, a}, {_, b} -> a > b end)
|> Enum.take(10)
```

Since Flow is based on GenStage, both libraries are compatible with each other. In fact, Flow processes can run independently as part of a supervision tree, and be part of a GenStage data-processing pipeline as well. This opens a range of possibilities and also means you don't have to worry about choosing one over the other—you can use both Flow and GenStage together. We are going to explore this in the next section.

Emitting Values from Reducers

 The on_trigger/2 function is not the only one that can control what values are emitted from the reducer stage. You can check emit/2 and emit_and_reduce/3 for more information.

Adding Flow to a GenStage Pipeline

We are going revisit the scraper project which we worked on in Chapter 3, Data-Processing Pipelines with GenStage, on page 57. To refresh your memory, the final data-processing pipeline we had for scraper had four components:

- One PageProducer process of type :producer
- Two OnlinePageConsumerProducer processes of type :producer_consumer
- One PageConsumerSupervisor process of type :consumer
- Up to two PageConsumer processes started on demand by PageConsumerSupervisor

To demonstrate how Flow works with GenStage, we are going to rewrite the original OnlinePageConsumerProducer implementation using Flow. When it comes to working with GenStage, there are two groups of functions available to use. The first group is made to work with already running stages:

- from_stages/2 to receive events from :producer stages

- through_stages/3 to send events to :producer_consumer stages and receive what they send in turn

- into_stages/3 to send events to :consumer or :producer_consumer stages

All functions in this group require a list of the process ids (PIDs) to connect to the already running processes.

The second group of functions is useful when you want Flow to start the GenStage processes for you. These are the functions:

- from_specs/2
- through_specs/3
- into_specs/3

They work exactly the same way as the ones in the previous group, except that they require a list of tuples instead of a list of PIDs. Each tuple represents a child specification, for example, {Module, args}, similar to the child specifications we use in supervisors. Flow uses the child specification to start the processes for you.

Our plan is to use from_stages/2 and into_stages/3 to connect to the already running PageProducer. We'll receive new page events, filter offline websites, and send them to PageConsumerSupervisor, just like before. Let's get started.

First, let's add flow to the scraper project:

```
scraper/mix.change1.exs
defp deps do
  [
    {:gen_stage, "~> 1.0"},
    {:flow, "~> 1.0"}
  ]
end
```

Next, replace the contents of OnlinePageProducerConsumer with this:

```
scraper/lib/online_page_producer_consumer.change2.ex
defmodule OnlinePageProducerConsumer do
  use Flow

  def start_link(_args) do
    producers = [Process.whereis(PageProducer)]

    consumers = [
      {Process.whereis(PageConsumerSupervisor), max_demand: 2}
    ]

    Flow.from_stages(producers, max_demand: 1, stages: 2)
    |> Flow.filter(&Scraper.online?/1)
    |> Flow.into_stages(consumers)
  end
end
```

This new version contains a lot less code than before. Let's break it down.

First, we replaced use GenStage with use Flow. We no longer need the via/1 and init/1 functions, so they are now gone. You will see why in just a moment. We have also removed the handle_events/3 callback, since Flow will manage that for us.

This leaves us with the start_link/1 function. Normally, you will start a Flow process Flow.start_link/2, similarly to GenStage.start_link/3. However, Flow.into_stages/3 will handle the start_link/2 logic for us.

We need the PID of PageProducer, so we used Process.whereis/1 to get it by name. This is then used by Flow.from_stages/2 to subscribe to the producer.

Previously, we used the Registry to name and start two instances of OnlinePage-ConsumerProducer. This is no longer needed, since we can set :stages to 2 in from_stages/2. This means that Flow will start two processes to manage the incoming workload. We also set :max_demand to 1 just like before, since the work we're doing is CPU intensive. This is why the via/1 function is no longer needed and can be safely removed.

Our business logic consists of filtering pages which are offline, which we achieve easily with Flow.filter/2.

Finally, we call the into_stages/3 function. It not only starts the process, similarly to Flow.start_link/2, but also dynamically subscribes PageConsumerSupervisor to OnlinePageConsumerProducer. We only had to pass the PID of the already running process and some options. However, this requires us to make some changes to the main application supervision tree:

```
scraper/lib/scraper/application.change5.ex
def start(_type, _args) do
  children = [
    PageProducer,
    PageConsumerSupervisor,
    OnlinePageProducerConsumer
  ]

  opts = [strategy: :one_for_one, name: Scraper.Supervisor]
  Supervisor.start_link(children, opts)
end
```

Since we are using Process.whereis/1 to get the PID of PageConsumerSupervisor, we have to make sure the process is started before OnlinePageConsumerProducer. We also no longer need the producer_consumer_spec/1 function, so we can remove that and add the process directly.

Finally, we need to explicitly set the :name argument when starting PageConsumer-Supervisor, since we're now using it to identify the process:

```
scraper/lib/page_consumer_supervisor.change3.ex
def start_link(_args) do
  ConsumerSupervisor.start_link(__MODULE__, :ok, name: __MODULE__)
end
```

The process no longer has to subscribe to anything when it starts, so let's update the options:

```
scraper/lib/page_consumer_supervisor.change3.ex
opts = [
  strategy: :one_for_one,
  subscribe_to: []
]
```

That's all we have to do to make it work. You'll need to run mix deps.get to download the new dependency, and then you can start IEx to test the changes:

```
22:59:08.198 [info]  PageProducer init
22:59:08.203 [info]  PageConsumerSupervisor init
22:59:08.208 [info]  Received demand for 1 pages
22:59:08.208 [info]  Received demand for 1 pages

iex(1)>
```

When the application starts, the two OnlinePageConsumerProducer processes started by Flow will issue a demand for one page event each. Now let's create some events and pass them to PageProducer:

```
iex(1)> pages = ["google.com", "facebook.com", "twitter.com",
  "amazon.com", "apple.com"]
["google.com", "facebook.com", "twitter.com", "amazon.com", "apple.com"]
iex(2)> PageProducer.scrape_pages(pages)
23:02:53.980 [info]  PageConsumer received facebook.com
23:02:55.982 [info]  PageConsumer received twitter.com
23:02:54.982 [info]  PageConsumer received amazon.com
23:02:55.982 [info]  Received demand for 1 pages
23:02:59.983 [info]  PageConsumer received apple.com
23:02:59.983 [info]  Received demand for 1 pages
```

Everything works just like before. Thanks to Flow, we simplified our code and made it a lot easier to understand. We almost didn't need any changes to other parts of the data-processing pipeline, other than removing obsolete code.

If you want to take this one step further, you can also remove PageConsumerSupervisor and do all the work required in OnlinePageConsumerProducer flow.

Now it's time for a recap.

Caution When Using into_stages/3 and through_stages/3

 Coordinating events and processes when using into_stages/3 and through_stages/3 could be complicated. If you are using them to process finite data, you have to be careful how processes exit—see the documentation for more information.[8,9]

Wrapping Up

When it comes to data-processing operations like map, filter, and reduce, there is no easier way to take advantage of GenStage than using Flow. At the same time, ease-of-use does not come at the expense of versatility. Most functions give you the option to configure the level of concurrency, events demand, and much more.

---

8. https://hexdocs.pm/flow/Flow.html#into_stages/3
9. https://hexdocs.pm/flow/Flow.html#through_stages/3

You may be tempted to replace all Enum and Stream module usage in your code with Flow. This is not a good idea. You get the best results from Flow only when you use it with large data sets or to perform hardware-intensive work. As you know, under the hood, Flow creates and manages a number of stage processes. While processes are lightweight, they are still an overhead when dealing with small tasks, which can be processed faster synchronously.

However, we covered a range of great use cases for Flow in this chapter. You optimized a CSV parsing function, first using the Stream module, and then using Flow to perform the data transformation concurrently. Then you saw how to partition data for reducer operations like reduce and group_by. We touched upon working with slow-running flows, where the same approach can be applied for unbounded streams of data. Finally, you integrated Flow into the GenStage data-processing pipeline in the scraper project, reducing the amount of code needed to process the data.

You can already use Flow to solve many challenging problems, but of course, there is still more to learn. The best way is to give Flow a try, and head over to the official documentation.

In the next chapter, we are going to look at Broadway. It is another popular library based on GenStage, which offers a convenient way to build data-ingestion pipelines that consume events from external message brokers, like RabbitMQ, Apache Kafka, Amazon SQS, and more.

CHAPTER 5

Data-Ingestion Pipelines with Broadway

Message brokers have been around for decades. Originally developed for large enterprises, they allowed software engineers to break down complex systems into independent services. The message broker would then act as a middleware between those services, effectively decoupling components that previously depended on each other. This significantly improved maintainability and made systems easier to scale to handle increased workloads.

Nowadays, message brokers are popular with companies and projects of any size and offer many advanced features. Most message brokers are open source and support all major operating systems. Others are proprietary software but still available at a low cost.

In this chapter, we're going to look at Broadway, an Elixir library that makes working with message brokers a breeze. Broadway, just like Flow, is built on top of GenStage. It makes it easy to build data-processing pipelines that consume events from external sources. This is why they are also called *data-ingestion pipelines*. Broadway supports the most popular message brokers and requires only a small amount of configuration to get up and running.

However, Broadway is not limited to working with just message brokers. In fact, it could be used with any existing GenStage producers. In many cases, this makes adopting GenStage a lot easier, since Broadway does the hard work of assembling the components of the pipeline.

Last but not least, the GenStage pipeline generated by Broadway is designed according to the current best practices. It is fault tolerant and performs graceful shutdowns out of the box, ensuring minimal loss of messages when something unexpected happens. It also has a number of other useful features, such as automatic acknowledgements, dynamic batching, rate limiting, and more. While you can certainly build this all yourself using GenStage, with Broadway you get everything with just a few lines of configuration code.

In this chapter, you're going to build a simple ticket-processing system. Along the way, you're going to learn about the Broadway behaviour and the callbacks that are available to implement. We will then move onto batch processing, which is another key feature that helps us process data efficiently and leverage concurrency. Finally, you will build your own Broadway producer using GenStage, and you will see how easy it is to use Broadway outside of the context of message brokers.

Let's get started!

Processing Ticketing Events

We're going to build an application that processes event messages sent by a legacy ticket booking system. Let's call it tickets. The legacy system publishes those events to a RabbitMQ message broker. We're going to use the messages to perform actions such as creating the ticket in the database and sending an email notification to the customer.

Our first task is to set up the project and make sure we have everything installed, so we can test new features locally.

First, you need to have RabbitMQ installed and running. You can follow the official instructions on the RabbitMQ website[1] to install it. If you have a choice of packages to use, select the one that contains the RabbitMQ Management plugin. Normally this plugin is included by default in most packages.

Once you have RabbitMQ installed and running, you should be able to open http://localhost:15672 in your browser to verify this. You will see the login page for the management panel. You can use the default username guest with password guest to log in.

Next, let's scaffold the tickets project:

```
$ mix new tickets --sup
```

Then change your current directory to the newly created folder with cd tickets.

We need to add broadway as a dependency. We also need the Broadway RabbitMQ producer, which is published as a separate package:

---

1. https://www.rabbitmq.com/download.html

tickets/mix.exs
```
defp deps do
  [
    {:broadway, "~> 0.6"},
    {:broadway_rabbitmq, "~> 0.6"}
  ]
end
```

Although we are using RabbitMQ for this project, most of the code will easily work with other message brokers. At the time of writing, Broadway officially supports the following message brokers:

- Amazon SQS via broadway_sqs
- Apache Kafka via broadway_kafka
- Google Cloud Pub/Sub via broadway_cloud_pub_sub
- RabbitMQ via broadway_rabbitmq, which is what we're using now

You can also find unofficial packages for Broadway on the Hex registry, which are prefixed with off_broadway_, for example off_broadway_redis for Redis.

Next, let's add :lager to extra_applications in mix.exs. This is an Erlang package used by one of the broadway_rabbitmq dependencies. You have to add it before the :logger application, otherwise you might see some harmless error messages in your logs:

tickets/mix.exs
```
def application do
  [
    extra_applications: [:lager, :logger],
    mod: {Tickets.Application, []}
  ]
end
```

This is specific to broadway_rabbitmq, so if you're using a different producer, you can skip this step.

Now you can run mix deps.get to download all dependencies.

We are ready to start building our data-ingestion pipeline. In order to use Broadway, you have to implement the Broadway behaviour, just like we've done before with GenServer and GenStage. However, Broadway comes with its own set of callbacks and configuration options. In the next section, we're going to add some functionality to tickets and start receiving messages from the message broker.

Broadway Callbacks In Depth

Now that we have the tickets project set up, we are ready to start writing some code. Once a message comes from the message broker, we want to use it to create a ticket in the database for the customer and send a confirmation email to them.

To accomplish this, we are going to use the Broadway behaviour to configure and start the data-ingestion pipeline. There are four callbacks available for us to implement:

- handle_message/3
- prepare_messages/2
- handle_failed/2
- handle_batch/4

In this section, we'll focus on the first three callbacks in the list. Don't worry, we're going to cover handle_batch/4 soon in Batching Messages, on page 127.

First, create a new file bookings_pipeline.ex in the lib folder. Then define the module BookingsPipeline like so:

```
defmodule BookingsPipeline do
  use Broadway

end
```

We also added use Broadway to bring in the Broadway behaviour.

Let's add the start_link/1 function next. Here is an outline of how the implementation looks:

```
def start_link(_args) do
  options = [
    name: BookingsPipeline,
    producer: [
      # ...
    ],
    processors: [
      # ...
    ]
  ]

  Broadway.start_link(__MODULE__, options)
end
```

As you can see, it's very similar to how start_link/1 works in other places.

The only exception is the keyword list of options. This is where all the configuration logic lives. Broadway uses this configuration to dynamically build and start all parts of the data-ingestion pipeline for us. The following configuration keys are required:

- :name, which Broadway uses as a prefix when naming processes
- :producer, which contains configuration about the source of events
- :processors, which allows us to configure the stage processes that receive the messages and do most of the work

However, the are many more settings available. We're going to look at the :batchers setting in Batching Messages, on page 127. For the full list of options, check the official documentation[2] for Broadway.start_link/2.

We're going to start simple, so let's use only the minimum required configuration to get started:

```
tickets/lib/bookings_pipeline.ex
@producer BroadwayRabbitMQ.Producer

@producer_config [
  queue: "bookings_queue",
  declare: [durable: true],
  on_failure: :reject_and_requeue
]

def start_link(_args) do
  options = [
    name: BookingsPipeline,
    producer: [module: {@producer, @producer_config}],
    processors: [
      default: []
    ]
  ]

  Broadway.start_link(__MODULE__, options)
end
```

Inside :producer, we must set the :module that will ask for messages. This module will manage the connection to the message broker for us. We have extracted the tuple values as the attributes @producer and @producer_config.

We set @producer to BroadwayRabbitMQ.Producer, which is a module that comes with the broadway_rabbitmq package.

In @producer_config we include broker-specific configuration. In this case, we want to connect to a queue called bookings_queue. The :declare option will create this queue in RabbitMQ if it doesn't exist already. Setting this to durable: true

---

2.   https://hexdocs.pm/broadway/Broadway.html#start_link/2

will persist the queue between broker restarts. Finally, we set the :on_failure setting to send failed messages back to the queue.

The @producer_config settings we use are specific to RabbitMQ, so if you're using a different message broker and producer, you must check its documentation. The supported options by broadway_rabbitmq are available here.[3]

After :producer we have the :processors key, which is also a keyword list. Inside, we set the :default key to an empty list. We are going to discuss processors in a moment, when we start implementing the handle_message/3 callback.

That's it, this is all that we need to get started with Broadway and the BroadwayRabbitMQ producer, and we only needed a few lines of code.

However, both the :producer and :processors settings offer a wide range of configuration options. For example, you can tweak the number of running producers and processors via the :concurrency key, like so:

```
producer: [
  module: {@producer, @producer_config}
  concurrency: 1
],
processors: [
  default: [
    concurrency: System.schedulers_online() * 2
  ]
]
```

In this example, we used the default values of 1 and System.schedulers_online() * 2. Since we're happy with the defaults, there is no need to add the :concurrency keys for BookingsPipeline. You can also set :min_demand and :max_demand in the :default keyword list, but again, we'll stick to their default values of 5 and 10.

You can find all available options for :producer and :processors in the Broadway documentation[4] and explore further what's possible.

Using this configuration, we will end up with a data-ingestion pipeline that works like the figure on page 119.

This is assuming you have two logical cores available. Not bad for just a few lines of code. However, the actual design of the pipeline is a lot more sophisticated than the figure shows and includes supervisors for fault tolerance as

---

3.   https://hexdocs.pm/broadway_rabbitmq/BroadwayRabbitMQ.Producer.html#module-options

4.   https://hexdocs.pm/broadway/Broadway.html#start_link/2-producers-options

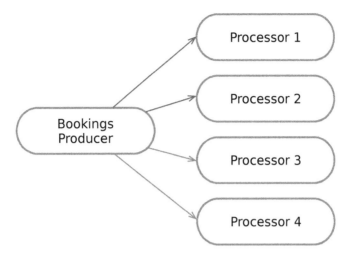

well as a mechanism to ensure graceful shutdowns. You can learn more about the underlying GenStage pipeline generated by Broadway here.[5]

The start_link/1 function is now complete, we just need to add BookingsPipeline to the application's supervision tree:

```
tickets/lib/tickets/application.ex
def start(_type, _args) do
  children = [
    BookingsPipeline
  ]

  opts = [strategy: :one_for_one, name: Tickets.Supervisor]
  Supervisor.start_link(children, opts)
end
```

Now we can move onto our first callback—handle_message/3.

Multiple Processors

 The :default group of processors is the only one that's allowed for now when configuring :processors. However, in the future, Broadway may support multiple processor groups.

Implementing handle_message/3

Incoming messages sent by the broker are processed by handle_message/3. Within this callback, you can look at the given message and its data and use it to perform any work.

---

5.   https://hexdocs.pm/broadway/architecture.html

The handle_message/3 callback is special. All callbacks that we've seen before, when using GenServer and GenStage, run within the current process. However, code written in handle_message/3 is executed by a *processor*. Processors are concurrently running processes started by Broadway to perform the work in handle_message/3. They also isolate any potential errors. If an exception happens, the pipeline will be restarted and quickly brought back to a working state.

There are three arguments given to handle_message/3:

- The current processor group, which is the atom :default for now
- The message itself, in the form of a %Broadway.Message{} struct
- The context value, which is optional, and available to set in start_link/2

The callback must return a %Broadway.Message{} struct. You will see what this struct contains in just a moment.

Let's implement handle_message/3 like so:

tickets/lib/bookings_pipeline.ex
```
def handle_message(_processor, message, _context) do
  # Add your business logic here...
  IO.inspect(message, label: "Message")
end
```

We are not doing anything special here, other than printing and returning the message.

Now we can finally run the tickets application with iex -S mix. You will see a bunch of information messages printed before the application starts, similar to this:

```
...
[info] Application rabbit_common started on node nonode@nohost
[info] Application amqp_client started on node nonode@nohost
[info] Application amqp started on node nonode@nohost
[info] Application nimble_options started on node nonode@nohost
[info] Application broadway_rabbitmq started on node nonode@nohost
...
```

Now let's go to http://localhost:15672/#/queues, and log in if you haven't already. The "Queues" tab shows the list of all queues, and you can see that bookings_queue has been created automatically as shown in the first screenshot on page 121.

Click on "bookings_queue" to go to this queue's dashboard. You will see a page with further information about the queue and some helpful tools.

Scroll down to the section "Publish message" and click on it to expand it. You should be able to see the payload text box and submit button as shown in the second screenshot on page 121.

We are going to use this to test our data-ingestion pipeline. The payload could be anything, but for simplicity, we'll use comma-separated values. The first value will be the type of event for the booking request, for example, musical, cinema, and so on. The second will be a numerical user identifier.

Enter musical,1 in the payload field, and click the "Publish message" submit button.

Now you can go back to your terminal where the application is running. You should see the incoming message printed in IEx:

```
Message: %Broadway.Message{
  acknowledger: {BroadwayRabbitMQ.Producer,
  %AMQP.Channel{
    conn: %AMQP.Connection{pid: #PID<0.339.0>},
    custom_consumer: nil,
```

```
      pid: #PID<0.351.0>
    },
    %{
      client: BroadwayRabbitMQ.AmqpClient,
      delivery_tag: 1,
      on_failure: :reject_and_requeue,
      on_success: :ack,
      redelivered: false
    }},
  batch_key: :default,
  batch_mode: :bulk,
  batcher: :default,
  data: "musical,1",
  metadata: %{
    amqp_channel: %AMQP.Channel{
      conn: %AMQP.Connection{pid: #PID<0.339.0>},
      custom_consumer: nil,
      pid: #PID<0.351.0>
    }
  },
  status: :ok
}
```

Congratulations, you just processed your first message. You can also see what the %Broadway.Message{} struct looks like. The payload that we just sent has been assigned to the :data field. The message also contains information about the pipeline itself and some useful metadata.

Now that we can receive messages, let's add some business logic next. We will create a couple of functions in the Tickets module. However, instead of writing the real logic, which will require setting up a database, we're going to use Process.sleep/1 and pretend that the database exists. This way we can focus on Broadway and keep things simple:

tickets/lib/tickets.ex
```elixir
def tickets_available?(_event) do
  Process.sleep(Enum.random(100..200))
  true
end

def create_ticket(_user, _event) do
  Process.sleep(Enum.random(250..1000))
end

def send_email(_user) do
  Process.sleep(Enum.random(100..250))
end

@users [
  %{id: "1", email: "foo@email.com"},
  %{id: "2", email: "bar@email.com"},
```

```
  %{id: "3", email: "baz@email.com"}
]
def users_by_ids(ids) when is_list(ids) do
  # Normally this would be a database query,
  # selecting only users whose id belongs to `ids`.
  Enum.filter(@users, & &1.id in ids)
end
```

Before creating a ticket, we want to make sure that tickets are still available, using the tickets_available?/1 function. If they are, we can insert the ticket record using create_ticket/2, and send a ticket confirmation email with send_email/1. The send_email/1 function expects a user argument, which should contain the email address to use.

To retrieve one or more users by ID, we added users_by_ids/1. As you can see, we are filtering a fixed list of users, which is our "database." Again, in a real-world application, you will probably use Ecto to perform a database query.

Before we send the confirmation email, we can fetch the user from the database, and pass it to send_email/1. However, if you do this in handle_message/3, there'll be a database request being made for each incoming message. This isn't ideal, especially if we're handling a lot of messages in a real production application.

When it comes to preloading data, the prepare_messages/2 callback is here to help.

Reducing Logs from BroadwayRabbitMQ

 The amqp client, which broadway_rabbitmq uses, could generate lots of debug messages. This debug output actually comes from :lager, which is similar to Elixir's Logger. You can refer to these instructions[6] if you'd like to turn off non-critical logs.

Implementing prepare_messages/2

It is very common to have to do some work in bulk when receiving messages. For example, you may want to fetch or preload information from the database. Rather than doing this in handle_message/3 for each message, you can run a single database query from prepare_messages/2.

The prepare_messages/2 callback runs before handle_message/3 and receives a *list* of messages. This means that you can iterate over the list, look at the data, and update it with more information. It also receives a user-defined context as the second argument, which we're going to ignore.

---

6. https://hexdocs.pm/amqp/readme.html#troubleshooting-faq

Let's implement prepare_messages/2 in BookingsPipeline:

tickets/lib/bookings_pipeline.ex
```elixir
def prepare_messages(messages, _context) do
  # Parse data and convert to a map.
  messages =
    Enum.map(messages, fn message ->
      Broadway.Message.update_data(message, fn data ->
        [event, user_id] = String.split(data, ",")
        %{event: event, user_id: user_id}
      end)
    end)

  users = Tickets.users_by_ids(Enum.map(messages, & &1.data.user_id))

  # Put users in messages.
  Enum.map(messages, fn message ->
    Broadway.Message.update_data(message, fn data ->
      user = Enum.find(users, & &1.id == data.user_id)
      Map.put(data, :user, user)
    end)
  end)
end
```

First, we parse the comma-separated values, and convert them to a map. Then we can collect the user ids, and fetch the users from the database. When updating message data, we can use the Message.update_data/2 helper. Finally, we have to make sure the prepare_messages/2 callback returns a list of messages back.

The customer data is now available, and we have the email address. We can update the handle_message/3 callback with the business logic:

```elixir
def handle_message(_processor, message, _context) do
  %{data: %{event: event, user: user}} = message

  # TODO: check for tickets availability.

  Tickets.create_ticket(user, event)
  Tickets.send_email(user)

  IO.inspect(message, label: "Message")
end
```

Now all business logic is in place. Let's restart the application, and head over to the RabbitMQ management panel. If you publish the same message as before—musical,1—you will get a slightly different output this time:

```
Message: %Broadway.Message{
  ...
  data: %{
    event: "musical",
```

```
    user: %{email: "foo@email.com", id: "1"},
    user_id: "1"
  },
  ...
}
```

Thanks to prepare_messages/2, the user information has been preloaded inside the message, and you can see that the :data field now contains a map with the user details.

Not all messages are meant to be successful. We still need to check whether tickets for a particular event are available or not. Let's say that all cinemas are temporarily closed, so we can no longer accept cinema bookings. If such a booking arrives, we should decline it and maybe take further action, for example, notifying the user by email. Let's see how we can do this next.

Caution When Using prepare_messages/2

 You should always keep your main business logic in handle_message/3 and use prepare_messages/2 only for preloading data. Also be careful with prepare_messages/2. A potential error in your code will cause all messages to be marked as failed.

Implementing handle_failed/3

Right now, when you return a message from handle_message/3, Broadway will automatically acknowledge it, since it has reached the end of the pipeline.

However, if an unhandled exception happens in your business logic, the message will be marked as failed. You can also manually mark a message as failed using Broadway.Message.failed/2. This could be useful when you want to discard messages that you don't want to process.

Remember that in @producer_config we configured the :on_failure setting with the value :reject_and_requeue. This means that failed messages will be sent back to RabbitMQ and redelivered. By default, messages will be redelivered indefinitely. We can change this setting to :reject_and_requeue_once or simply :reject to completely discard all failed messages.

We can also configure acknowledgements on a per-message basis, and the ideal place for that is handle_failed/3. The optional handle_failed/3 callback gives us the ability to check what messages have failed and why and decide if we want to take further action.

Let's update the tickets_available?/1 function and pattern match for cinema events. We will return false to all of them for being unavailable:

```elixir
def tickets_available?("cinema") do
  Process.sleep(Enum.random(100..200))
  false
end

def tickets_available?(_event) do
  Process.sleep(Enum.random(100..200))
  true
end
```

We can then use the function in handle_message/3 to check each message:

tickets/lib/bookings_pipeline.change1.ex
```elixir
def handle_message(_processor, message, _context) do
  %{data: %{event: event, user: user}} = message

  if Tickets.tickets_available?(event) do
    Tickets.create_ticket(user, event)
    Tickets.send_email(user)
    IO.inspect(message, label: "Message")
  else
    Broadway.Message.failed(message, "bookings-closed")
  end
end
```

Broadway.Message.failed/2 lets you specify the reason why the message has failed. This is useful because it helps you to decide what to do with the message later.

Now we can implement handle_failed/2. When a message fails with the reason "bookings-closed", we will discard it, otherwise we will keep retrying. This is how it works:

tickets/lib/bookings_pipeline.change1.ex
```elixir
def handle_failed(messages, _context) do
  IO.inspect(messages, label: "Failed messages")

  Enum.map(messages, fn
    %{status: {:failed, "bookings-closed"}} = message ->
      Broadway.Message.configure_ack(message, on_failure: :reject)

    message ->
      message
  end)
end
```

Notice that we use the Broadway.Message.configure_ack/2 helper to overwrite the acknowledgment setting for the message.

When you restart the application, you can try publishing a message with payload cinema,2. You should see this in IEx:

```
Failed messages: [
  %Broadway.Message{
    ...
    data: %{
      event: "cinema",
      user: %{email: "bar@email.com", id: "2"},
      user_id: "2"
    },
    ...
    status: {:failed, "bookings-closed"}
  }
]
```

That's perfect. We rejected the failed messages, while others will be requeued and retried as normal.

It is useful to know that when a message fails due an error, the :status field value will be {:error, error, stacktrace}.

Messages often fail due to an error in our logic, which can happen in other places, not just handle_message/3. For example, if preprocessing fails in prepare_messages/2, the whole group of messages will be marked as failed. The same thing applies when working with batches. In all cases, you'll have a chance to see what's going on using the handle_failed/2 callback.

You just built your first data-ingestion pipeline! You got highly concurrent processing for free, thanks to the built-in processors, and added some useful features such as data preloading and per-message error handling.

All of this is great, but there is another important feature in Broadway that we haven't explored yet, and this feature is batching.

Configuring RabbitMQ Queues

 If you use the :reject_and_requeue setting, messages will be redelivered indefinitely. You can put a limit on retries by configuring the time to live (TTL) for messages using a policy, or use a dead-letter queue. You can check the RabbitMQ documentation[7] for more information.

Batching Messages

Using processors is great for many tasks, but sometimes you will need another layer of stages. Your business logic in handle_message/3 could become

---

7. https://www.rabbitmq.com/ttl.html

a bottleneck and slow down the pipeline, especially under heavy workloads. You may also want to improve efficiency by grouping and running some operations together. This is where batching comes in to help.

Using batching in Broadway is an easy way to add another step in your data-ingestion pipeline for further processing. It allows you to leverage concurrency, and group relevant messages together to perform operations in bulk. In this section, we're going to configure batching for BookingsPipeline to improve how tickets are being created. Rather than inserting tickets in the database one by one, we will group them together, and perform a single "insert all" operation.

But first, we need a way to quickly create and send messages from RabbitMQ. Using the Management panel to send a lot of messages by hand is going to be too cumbersome.

Instead, let's use the amqp package. AMQP stands for *Advanced Message Queuing Protocol*, which is an open standard protocol used by RabbitMQ. The amqp client, which broadway_rabbitmq uses internally, can help us publish messages to bookings_queue programatically.

Let's add the amqp package to our dependencies:

```
tickets/mix.change1.exs
defp deps do
  [
    {:broadway, "~> 0.6"},
    {:broadway_rabbitmq, "~> 0.6"},
    {:amqp, "~> 1.6"}
  ]
end
```

Then create the file .iex.exs at the top-level project directory, and add the following:

```
tickets/.iex.exs
send_messages = fn num_messages ->
  {:ok, connection} = AMQP.Connection.open()
  {:ok, channel} = AMQP.Channel.open(connection)

  Enum.each(1..num_messages, fn _ ->
    event = Enum.random(["cinema", "musical", "play"])
    user_id = Enum.random(1..3)
    AMQP.Basic.publish(channel, "", "bookings_queue", "#{event},#{user_id}")
  end)

  AMQP.Connection.close(connection)
end
```

We've assigned a function to send_messages, which takes a single argument—the number of test messages to send. We are using AMQP.Connection.open/1 to connect to the RabbitMQ server, using the default port and credentials. Once you have the connection, you can open a *channel* and start publishing messages to a queue.

We use Enum.random/1 to randomize the message data, so we should get a mix of events of type musical, cinema, and play, booked by different users.

Finally, let's remove this code that we added previously in tickets.ex:

```
def tickets_available?("cinema") do
  Process.sleep(Enum.random(100..200))
  false
end
```

We used this to demonstrate how handle_failed/2 works, but we won't need it from now on. We want to let all messages succeed and go through the pipeline.

You can restart the tickets application and see the new code in action. Since we assigned a function to a local variable, we need to use the dot syntax when calling it:

```
iex(1)> send_messages.(2)
:ok

Message: %Broadway.Message{
  ...
  data: %{
    event: "play",
    user: %{email: "baz@email.com", id: "3"},
    user_id: "3"
  },
  ...
}
Message: %Broadway.Message{
  ...
  data: %{
    event: "musical",
    user: %{email: "bar@email.com", id: "2"},
    user_id: "2"
  },
  ...
}
```

Everything works correctly, and we can start working on our new feature.

Implementing Batching and handle_batch/4

The tickets application currently handles several types of events and creates records in the database for each one. We are going to use batching to group the incoming events by type and insert them all together.

To start using batching, we need to add a bit of configuration to enable it. We can then implement the handle_batch/4 callback, which is the last callback on our list.

Just like handle_message/3, handle_batch/4 is special, and all code within the callback runs concurrently in a separate *batch processor*. Batching works by configuring one or more *batchers*. Each batcher will start a single batch processor by default, which runs the code in handle_batch/4 to process the given group of messages.

Let's add the :batchers key first:

tickets/lib/bookings_pipeline.change2.ex
```
options = [
  name: BookingsPipeline,
  producer: [module: {@producer, @producer_config}],
  processors: [
    default: []
  ],
  batchers: [
    default: []
  ]
]
```

Adding the :batchers key will instruct Broadway to extend the pipeline.

Just like :processors, you can configure :batchers in different ways, but let's leave it as it is for now. We'll revisit this part in a bit when we configure batching by event type.

Next is the handle_batch/4 callback:

tickets/lib/bookings_pipeline.change2.ex
```
def handle_batch(_batcher, messages, batch_info, _context) do
  IO.inspect(batch_info, label: "#{inspect(self())} Batch")

  messages
end
```

The handle_batch/4 callback receives the current batcher (which will be :default in this case) and the list of messages in the batch. It also gets a %BatchInfo{} struct and the optional user-defined context. Let's see what's in the batch information struct by inspecting it with IO.inspect/2.

At the end of the callback, we must return all messages. You can still mark some messages as failed at this stage, otherwise Broadway will automatically acknowledge all of them as successful.

Now we can restart the tickets application, and use the send_messages/1 helper to send 500 test events:

```
iex(1)> send_messages.(500)
...
#PID<0.339.0> Batch: %Broadway.BatchInfo{
  batch_key: :default,
  batcher: :default,
  partition: nil,
  size: 50
}
#PID<0.339.0> Batch: %Broadway.BatchInfo{
  ...
  size: 43
}
#PID<0.339.0> Batch: %Broadway.BatchInfo{
  ...
  size: 39
}
...
```

You can see the %BatchInfo{} structs being printed in IEx as the batches are being processed. The struct has a few fields:

- :batcher is the batcher group and belongs to one of the groups defined in start_link/1.

- :batch_key is an identifier for a group of a messages within the batch.

- :partition is the partition key, if partitioning is configured (this is an optional feature).

- :size is the number of messages in the batch.

Batching seems to be working, so now we can take advantage of it. We will move some of the logic in handle_message/3 to handle_batch/4. The plan is to let handle_message/3 check for tickets availability, and then let the batch processor create the tickets in the database. This way, we can insert new tickets in bulk and increase the overall performance.

Using Static Batching

Each message returned by the handle_message/3 callback must belong to a batcher. If one hasn't been assigned, messages will go to the :default batcher. This is the group we have defined already in start_link/1, so everything just worked for us and we didn't need to do anything.

Unlike :processors, the :batchers configuration supports multiple groups. This means that you can have more than one batcher doing the work. We can use this to create batchers per event type. For example, we can have a :cinema batcher and a :musical batcher for cinema and musical bookings, while all other events go to the :default group. We call this *static batching*, since batcher groups are hard coded and are part of the pipeline configuration.

Let's add some more batchers to our pipeline:

```
tickets/lib/bookings_pipeline.change3.ex
options = [
  name: BookingsPipeline,
  producer: [module: {@producer, @producer_config}],
  processors: [
    default: []
  ],
  batchers: [
    cinema: [],
    musical: [],
    default: []
  ]
]
```

Now we can use Broadway.Message.put_batcher/2 to assign a batcher to each message. This is our updated handle_message/3 function:

```
tickets/lib/bookings_pipeline.change3.ex
def handle_message(_processor, message, _context) do
  if Tickets.tickets_available?(message.data.event) do
    case message do
      %{data: %{event: "cinema"}} = message ->
        Broadway.Message.put_batcher(message, :cinema)

      %{data: %{event: "musical"}} = message ->
        Broadway.Message.put_batcher(message, :musical)

      message ->
        message
    end
  else
    Broadway.Message.failed(message, "bookings-closed")
  end
end
```

As we said earlier, we'll move ticket creation to the batch processor, but we need a way to insert multiple tickets at once. Again, we'll add some dummy code to the Tickets module and use it to slow processing down:

tickets/lib/tickets.ex
```elixir
def insert_all_tickets(messages) do
  # Normally `Repo.insert_all/3` if using `Ecto`...
  Process.sleep(Enum.count(messages) * 250)
  messages
end
```

Our new handle_batch/4 function will now look like this:

tickets/lib/bookings_pipeline.change3.ex
```elixir
def handle_batch(_batcher, messages, batch_info, _context) do
  IO.puts("#{inspect(self())} Batch #{batch_info.batcher}
    #{batch_info.batch_key}"))

  messages
  |> Tickets.insert_all_tickets()
  |> Enum.each(fn %{data: %{user: user}} ->
    Tickets.send_email(user)
  end)

  messages
end
```

We've added some debug output so we can see the process identifier and the current :batcher and :batch_key values in batch_info. Then we use the messages and their data to insert the records in the database. Once that's done, we have to send the email confirmation for each booking, just like before.

Let's try this out with another 500 messages. You'll start seeing output similar to this in IEx:

```
#PID<0.347.0> Batch default default
```
```
#PID<0.339.0> Batch cinema default
```
```
#PID<0.339.0> Batch cinema default
```
```
#PID<0.343.0> Batch musical default
```
```
#PID<0.339.0> Batch cinema default
```

. . .

You can see the batcher groups being used, which means everything works as expected. The process identifier printed before each message is the one of the batch processor doing the work. By default, you get one batch processor per batcher, but you can increase this by using the :concurrency key on each batcher group.

Batching also makes it easier to run custom logic for each batcher if you need to do so. For example, imagine that cinema bookings are made to a separate database and need special logic. You can easily pattern match on the batcher value in handle_batch/3, to organize your code:

```
def handle_batch(:cinema, messages, batch_info, _context) do
  # Process cinema bookings...
end

def handle_batch(_batcher, messages, batch_info, _context) do
  # Process all other bookings...
end
```

In the debug output, we also included the :batch_key value for each %BatchInfo{} struct, but we haven't talked about it yet. Looking at the output, this value is always :default, regardless of the batch. Batch key is in fact quite useful, so we're going to look into it in detail in the next section.

Using Dynamic Batching

Using static batching is great when you know how to group your messages in advance. But often, messages contain dynamic data, which means that static batching is not going to work. Thankfully, Broadway gives us the option to define batches at runtime using :batch_key. This is also called *dynamic batching*.

To use dynamic batching, you can set :batch_key on the message using Broadway.Message.put_batch_key/2 in your handle_message/3 callback. The batch key is then used to partition the data within each batch for each batcher group.

We can demonstrate how dynamic batching works by improving our email notifications. Right now, if a user does multiple bookings, they will get multiple emails. This is going to be annoying for all customers, and it will also increase our bill from the email service provider.

Instead, let's batch ticket confirmations, and send a single email to the customer. We're going to group notifications by email address, and also prevent sending too many emails at once, by introducing a ten-second window.

To accomplish this, we'll create another pipeline called NotificationsPipeline. Create the file notifications_pipeline.ex in the lib directory, and add the following logic:

```
tickets/lib/notifications_pipeline.ex
defmodule NotificationsPipeline do
  use Broadway

  @producer BroadwayRabbitMQ.Producer

  @producer_config [
    queue: "notifications_queue",
    declare: [durable: true],
    on_failure: :reject_and_requeue,
    qos: [prefetch_count: 100]
  ]
```

```elixir
  def start_link(_args) do
    options = [
      name: NotificationsPipeline,
      producer: [module: {@producer, @producer_config}],
      processors: [
        default: []
      ],
      batchers: [
        email: [concurrency: 5, batch_timeout: 10_000],
      ]
    ]

    Broadway.start_link(__MODULE__, options)
  end

  def handle_message(_processor, message, _context) do
    message
    |> Broadway.Message.put_batcher(:email)
    |> Broadway.Message.put_batch_key(message.data.recipient)
  end

  def prepare_messages(messages, _context) do
    Enum.map(messages, fn message ->
      Broadway.Message.update_data(message, fn data ->
        [type, recipient] = String.split(data, ",")
        %{type: type, recipient: recipient}
      end)
    end)
  end

  def handle_batch(_batcher, messages, batch_info, _context) do
    IO.puts("#{inspect(self())} Batch #{batch_info.batcher}
      #{batch_info.batch_key}")

    # Send an email digest to the user with all information.

    messages
  end
end
```

Most of this code should be now familiar to you. We're connecting to a new RabbitMQ queue called notifications_queue. We use the comma-separated values format, and the expected values are two: the type of notification (such as email), followed by the recipient (for example foo@email.com). We're keeping this flexible, so we can add more types of notifications in the future.

We configured a single batcher called :email, with five batch processors. We're also using the setting batch_timeout, which we haven't seen before. We're going to discuss :batch_timeout in more detail in a moment. For now, you just need to know that we're introducing a window of ten seconds for sending an email to a recipient.

Although we have a single batcher, we're using Broadway.Message.put_batch_key/2 for dynamic batching. Broadway will use the recipient value to partition incoming data.

Let's add NotificationsPipeline to the application's supervision tree:

```
tickets/lib/tickets/application.change1.ex
def start(_type, _args) do
  children = [
    BookingsPipeline,
    NotificationsPipeline
  ]

  opts = [strategy: :one_for_one, name: Tickets.Supervisor]
  Supervisor.start_link(children, opts)
end
```

Finally, we will update BookingsPipeline and make it enqueue notifications back to the message broker as soon as it is done processing a batch of tickets. Thanks to BroadwayRabbitMQ.Producer, we have a channel open to the RabbitMQ server, included in the message metadata. We can use it to publish a message using AMQP:

```
tickets/lib/bookings_pipeline.change4.ex
def handle_batch(_batcher, messages, batch_info, _context) do
  IO.puts("#{inspect(self())} Batch #{batch_info.batcher}
    #{batch_info.batch_key}")

  messages
  |> Tickets.insert_all_tickets()
  |> Enum.each(fn message ->
    channel = message.metadata.amqp_channel
    payload = "email,#{message.data.user.email}"
    AMQP.Basic.publish(channel, "", "notifications_queue", payload)
  end)

  messages
end
```

Let's restart the application and send another 500 messages. You'll start seeing something like this:

```
#PID<0.334.0> Batch musical default
#PID<0.341.0> Batch default default
#PID<0.328.0> Batch cinema default
#PID<0.333.0> Batch musical default

...

#PID<0.389.0> Batch email foo@email.com
#PID<0.390.0> Batch email baz@email.com
#PID<0.391.0> Batch email bar@email.com

...
```

Watching the output, you'll see emails being sent, at most, only once every ten seconds. This is a great improvement over our previous implementation.

Of course, we oversimplified our notifications on purpose. Normally we'll need the notification text and other variables in the message, so we can include them in the email. We also skipped the logic that creates the digest email before sending it. This could be a fun project to work on once you complete this chapter. You can also try adding support for other notifications such as text or instant messages.

Other than :batcher and :batch_key, there two more variables which determine how batching works. You already saw :batch_timeout, which we used for NotificationsPipeline. The other is variable is :batch_size. We're going to have a quick look at them next.

Adjusting Batch Size and Timeout

If you inspect batch_info.size in the handle_batch/4 callbacks, you will notice that our batches contain no more than fifty messages. The maximum number of received messages is also known as *batch size* and is typically controlled by the :batch_size value for each batcher in start_link/1, like so:

```
...
batchers: [
  ...
  default: [
    batch_size: 100
  ]
]
```

However, the default value for :batch_size for each batcher is already 100. It may seem like something is going wrong, since we're only getting half the expected amount.

This is actually by design and is specific to the broadway_rabbitmq producer. The BroadwayRabbitMQ.Producer module maintains an active connection to the RabbitMQ server, which allows it to receive messages as soon as they get in the queue. This is why it sets a limit on the number of messages coming from RabbitMQ, so it can control the flow and handle back-pressure. This is documented in the official broadway_rabbitmq documentation page.[8]

The good news is that you can easily increase this limit by passing some extra configuration to your producer config:

---

8. https://hexdocs.pm/broadway_rabbitmq/BroadwayRabbitMQ.Producer.html#module-back-pressure-and-prefetch_count

```
@producer_config [
  queue: "bookings_queue",
  declare: [durable: true],
  on_failure: :reject_and_requeue,
  qos: [prefetch_count: 100]
]
```

Here we set :prefetch_count to 100, which is the same as the default value for :batch_size.

Now you can tweak :batch_size per batcher, and each will be able to receive up to 100 messages:

```
...
batchers: [
  cinema: [batch_size: 75],
  musical: [], # defaults to :batch_size of 100
  default: [batch_size: 50]
]
```

You may ask what happens when there are less than the required number of messages available. The batcher will only wait a certain amount of time to reach the configured :batch_size. After this, it will just send the available messages for processing and start again. This is controlled by the :batch_timeout setting.

The default value for :batch_timeout is 1000 milliseconds, but you can change it like we did in NotificationsPipeline:

```
...
batchers: [
  email: [concurrency: 5, batch_timeout: 10_000]
]
```

It's important to note that :batch_size and :batch_timeout work *per batch key*. This means that these four variables—:batcher, :batch_key, :batch_size, and :batch_time-out—ultimately determine what messages the batch processors receive. Choosing the right settings comes down to each use case, so you have to find the right combination to ensure efficient flow of messages through the pipeline.

We've covered quite a few features already. You've seen that a few lines of configuration and implementing a handful of callbacks go a long way. In the next section, we're going to see that Broadway works great not just with message brokers, but also with custom producers.

Using GenStage Producers

Broadway is an excellent choice when working with popular message brokers. However, it's not limited to just that. Broadway could be useful in a wide range of use cases where you need a data-processing pipeline with dynamic batching built-in. All you have to do is bring your own GenStage producer, and Broadway will happily do the work for you. We're going to see how this works by revisiting the scraper project one last time. We already used GenStage and Flow to implement it, so it will be great to have another version implemented using Broadway, for comparison.

Let's start by replacing :flow with :broadway in the dependencies list:

```
scraper/mix.change2.exs
defp deps do
  [
    {:gen_stage, "~> 1.0"},
    {:broadway, "~> 0.6"}
  ]
end
```

We are going to use the built-in processors in Broadway to do the heavy lifting, leverage concurrency, and provide. This means that we no longer need Online PageProducerConsumer, PageConsumerSupervisor, and PageConsumer. You can delete their files later so they don't get in the way. Everything they do will be replaced by the brand new ScrapingPipeline.

Let's create the file scraping_pipeline.ex in the lib directory, and define it like so:

```
defmodule ScrapingPipeline do
  use Broadway
  require Logger

end
```

ScrapingPipeline is going to be responsible for starting all parts of the pipeline, including the producer. You're going to see how we're going to use PageProducer in a moment, but first, let's update the applications.ex file:

```
scraper/lib/scraper/application.change6.ex
def start(_type, _args) do
  children = [
    ScrapingPipeline
  ]
  opts = [strategy: :one_for_one, name: Scraper.Supervisor]
  Supervisor.start_link(children, opts)
end
```

Now let's start working on the pipeline configuration in ScrapingPipeline. We are going to use the PageProducer module, like so:

```
def start_link(_args) do
  options = [
    name: ScrapingPipeline,
    producer: [
      module: {PageProducer, []},
      transformer: {ScrapingPipeline, :transform, []}
    ],
    processors: [
      default: []
    ]
  ]

  Broadway.start_link(__MODULE__, options)
end
```

For the :module tuple in the :producer list, we use the PageProducer module, with no arguments. Broadway will use this to start PageProducer as part of the pipeline. We are also using a new setting in :producer which you haven't seen before, called :transformer.

As you saw when using BroadwayRabbitMQ.Producer, Broadway messages are wrapped in %Message{} structs. However, PageProducer emits events that are just strings, such as "twitter.com".

We have two options: we can either update PageProducer to emit %Message{} structs, or use the :transformer setting. We opted for the latter.

The :transformer setting accepts a module-function-arguments (MFA) tuple, which will be used to convert incoming events to %Message{} structs. Let's implement it:

scraper/lib/scraping_pipeline.ex
```
def transform(event, _options) do
  %Broadway.Message{
    data: event,
    acknowledger: {ScrapingPipeline, :pages, []}
  }
end
```

Other than setting the event value as the :data, we are also setting an *acknowledger*. The acknowledger receives groups of messages that have been processed, successfully or not. This is usually an opportunity to contact the message broker and inform it of the outcome. But in this case, PageProducer doesn't really care if a message has been processed or not. That's why we can implement the acknowledger like this:

scraper/lib/scraping_pipeline.ex
```
def ack(:pages, _successful, _failed) do
  :ok
end
```

The ack/3 receives the acknowledger id, which we previously defined as :pages in the transform/2 function. It also gets two lists, containing the successful and failed messages. Right now we just return :ok regardless of the outcome for each message. Perhaps in the future, if PageProducer has an internal queue, we can send messages back to be retried.

As we said earlier, ScrapingPipeline will now take ownership of PageProducer. We need to make one change to ensure its API works just as before.

Updating PageProducer

Since ScrapingPipeline is starting the process for us, we no longer need the start_link/2 function in PageProducer, so we can delete it.

We also need to update the scrape_pages/1 function. Right now it looks like this:

```
def scrape_pages(pages) when is_list(pages) do
  GenStage.cast(__MODULE__, {:pages, pages})
end
```

However, sending a message to __MODULE__ will no longer work. When Broadway starts processes, it gives them names based on the name of the pipeline and their role. Each process also has an index added to their name. As a result, the name of the GenStage process is no longer equivalent to the __MODULE__ name.

To fix this, we need to find out what the producer is called. We can use the Broadway.producer_names/1 helper to do that. For example, running it in the tickets project will give you this result:

```
iex> Broadway.producer_names(BookingsPipeline)

[BookingsPipeline.Broadway.Producer_0]
```

As you can see, there is one producer process running.

Let's use producer_names/2 to fix scrape_pages/1':

```
scraper/lib/page_producer.change2.ex
def scrape_pages(pages) when is_list(pages) do
  ScrapingPipeline
  |> Broadway.producer_names()
  |> List.first()
  |> GenStage.cast({:pages, pages})
end
```

The PageProducer integration is now complete. Next, we need to think about bringing the old processing logic over to ScrapingPipeline. We need two processes; each will then check if the given page is online and then forward only working pages to the final step of the pipeline. Let's do this next.

Configuring ScrapingPipeline

We're going to use Broadway's processors to refactor the logic which checks each website. All we have to do is define :processors in start_link/1, and use han-dle_message/3:

```
def start_link(_args) do
  options = [
    name: ScrapingPipeline,
    producer: [
      module: {PageProducer, []},
      transformer: {ScrapingPipeline, :transform, []}
    ],
    processors: [
      default: [max_demand: 1, concurrency: 2]
    ]
  ]

  Broadway.start_link(__MODULE__, options)
end

def handle_message(_processor, message, _context) do
  if Scraper.online?(message.data) do
    # To do...
  else
    Broadway.Message.failed(message, "offline")
  end
end
```

We can discard offline websites using Broadway.Message.failed/2. Messages that are successful go to the next step, which would do the "scraping" work.

This is where Broadway's batchers will come in handy. To maintain our previous logic, we're going define a batcher with :batch_size set to 1, and two batch processors, like so:

```
scraper/lib/scraping_pipeline.ex
processors: [
  default: [max_demand: 1, concurrency: 2]
],
batchers: [
  default: [batch_size: 1, concurrency: 2],
]
```

When doing web scraping, we don't want to send too many requests to a single website and cause a surge in traffic. We can use Broadway's dynamic batching to ensure that potential URLs to the same domain are grouped together for scraping. We could parse and extract the domain name from each message and use that for dynamic batching. For now, we'll just use the entire page address, to keep things simple:

```
scraper/lib/scraping_pipeline.ex
def handle_message(_processor, message, _context) do
  if Scraper.online?(message.data) do
    Broadway.Message.put_batch_key(message, message.data)
  else
    Broadway.Message.failed(message, "offline")
  end
end
```

The final piece of the puzzle is the handle_batch/4 logic:

```
scraper/lib/scraping_pipeline.ex
def handle_batch(_batcher, [message], _batch_info, _context) do
  Logger.info("Batch Processor received #{message.data}")
  Scraper.work()
  [message]
end
```

Right now it gets a single message to scrape one page at a time.

That's it. Let's start up the application and give it a go:

```
16:38:30.514 [info]  PageProducer init

16:38:30.520 [info]  Received demand for 1 pages

16:38:30.520 [info]  Received demand for 1 pages

iex(1)> pages = ["google.com", "facebook.com", "twitter.com",
  "amazon.com", "apple.com"]
["google.com", "facebook.com", "twitter.com", "amazon.com", "apple.com"]

iex(2)> PageProducer.scrape_pages(pages)
:ok

16:39:34.235 [info]  Batch Processor received google.com

16:39:34.235 [info]  Batch Processor received facebook.com

16:39:38.236 [info]  Received demand for 1 pages

16:39:38.238 [info]  Received demand for 1 pages

16:39:39.236 [info]  Batch Processor received apple.com
```

Everything seems to work as expected. We are converting incoming events so Broadway can process them, then filtering offline pages concurrently using the processors. Finally, we limited the number of scrapers running in parallel by configuring how batchers work. Most importantly, you saw how you can use custom GenStage producers with Broadway, which should also help you understand how existing packages like broadway_rabbitmq work.

Broadway producers also get some extra callbacks, so they can integrate even better with the rest of the pipeline. They are prepare_for_start/2 and prepare_for_draining/2, which run when the pipeline starts and stops, respectively. You can read more about them here.[9]

Now it's time for a recap.

Wrapping Up

In this chapter, you learned about Broadway, which not only simplifies working with message brokers but also takes away the complexity of assembling data-processing pipelines. We configured our pipeline to connect to a RabbitMQ server and consume events. We used processors to perform work concurrently and batchers to do further processing in bulk. Finally, you saw how to make your own producer from scratch, which showed you how versatile Broadway can be.

There are even more features in Broadway that we didn't explore in this book but are well documented online. Examples include rate limiting, partitioning, and metrics exposed using the telemetry library. There are also various helpers that make testing Broadway pipelines easy. I encourage you to check the official documentation to learn more.[10]

You have completed the final chapter in this book, and by now, you know about the most important tools available in Elixir to build high-performance, highly concurrent applications. Thanks to Erlang and the BEAM, Elixir has always benefited from an excellent concurrency model and a battle-tested foundation. After years of development, Elixir has also come up with its own abstractions that have built upon this foundation. As Elixir engineers, we have the luxury of choosing between several high-quality libraries that are easy to scale to handle any amount of traffic. Let's review your options.

Whenever you want to perform work concurrently without much hassle, you can use the Task module. Using Task.async_stream/3 is a great way to process large collections of data and provide back-pressure at the same time.

However, complex tasks often need to maintain their own state and run over long periods of time. This is where GenServer comes in handy. You can use it to create processes that you can interact with, and solve harder problems.

Sometimes the amount of concurrent work that you have to perform is variable, and you are at risk of exhausting your system resources. For example,

---

9. https://hexdocs.pm/broadway/Broadway.Producer.html
10. https://hexdocs.pm/broadway

surges of traffic frequently bring even the largest web services offline, because they are unable to allocate resources to handle the increased traffic. GenStage enables you to create complex data-processing pipelines that are resilient by controlling consumer demand and handling back-pressure.

Flow helps you aggregate data by leveraging GenStage under the hood. If you are working with big datasets and you're filtering, mapping, and reducing data, then this is probably the best tool for you to use.

Finally, Broadway fills an important gap when building data-ingestion pipelines that consume external events. You can use it not only with message brokers but also to build robust event-processing systems.

This was a quick overview of everything that you have learned so far. This might be the end of the book, but your journey has just begun. Now that you have completed this book, you can build even faster, more resilient applications in Elixir, and focus on solving any challenges that may arise along the way. Good luck!

Bibliography

[Tho18]   Dave Thomas. *Programming Elixir 1.6*. The Pragmatic Bookshelf, Raleigh, NC, 2018.

Index

Thank you!

How did you enjoy this book? Please let us know. Take a moment and email us at support@pragprog.com with your feedback. Tell us your story and you could win free ebooks. Please use the subject line "Book Feedback."

Ready for your next great Pragmatic Bookshelf book? Come on over to https://pragprog.com and use the coupon code BUYANOTHER2021 to save 30% on your next ebook.

Void where prohibited, restricted, or otherwise unwelcome. Do not use ebooks near water. If rash persists, see a doctor. Doesn't apply to *The Pragmatic Programmer* ebook because it's older than the Pragmatic Bookshelf itself. Side effects may include increased knowledge and skill, increased marketability, and deep satisfaction. Increase dosage regularly.

And thank you for your continued support.

The Pragmatic Bookshelf

Designing Elixir Systems with OTP

You know how to code in Elixir; now learn to think in it. Learn to design libraries with intelligent layers that shape the right data structures, flow from one function into the next, and present the right APIs. Embrace the same OTP that's kept our telephone systems reliable and fast for over 30 years. Move beyond understanding the OTP functions to knowing what's happening under the hood, and why that matters. Using that knowledge, instinctively know how to design systems that deliver fast and resilient services to your users, all with an Elixir focus.

James Edward Gray, II and Bruce A. Tate
(246 pages) ISBN: 9781680506617. $41.95
https://pragprog.com/book/jgotp

Functional Web Development with Elixir, OTP, and Phoenix

Elixir and Phoenix are generating tremendous excitement as an unbeatable platform for building modern web applications. For decades OTP has helped developers create incredibly robust, scalable applications with unparalleled uptime. Make the most of them as you build a stateful web app with Elixir, OTP, and Phoenix. Model domain entities without an ORM or a database. Manage server state and keep your code clean with OTP Behaviours. Layer on a Phoenix web interface without coupling it to the business logic. Open doors to powerful new techniques that will get you thinking about web development in fundamentally new ways.

Lance Halvorsen
(218 pages) ISBN: 9781680502435. $45.95
https://pragprog.com/book/lhelph

Hands-on Rust

Rust is an exciting new programming language combining the power of C with memory safety, fearless concurrency, and productivity boosters—and what better way to learn than by making games. Each chapter in this book presents hands-on, practical projects ranging from "Hello, World" to building a full dungeon crawler game. With this book, you'll learn game development skills applicable to other engines, including Unity and Unreal.

Herbert Wolverson
(342 pages) ISBN: 9781680508161. $47.95
https://pragprog.com/book/hwrust

Modern Front-End Development for Rails

Improve the user experience for your Rails app with rich, engaging client-side interactions. Learn to use the Rails 6 tools and simplify the complex JavaScript ecosystem. It's easier than ever to build user interactions with Hotwire, Turbo, Stimulus, and Webpacker. You can add great front-end flair without much extra complication. Use React to build a more complex set of client-side features. Structure your code for different levels of client-side needs with these powerful options. Add to your toolkit today!

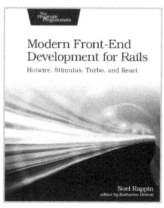

Noel Rappin
(396 pages) ISBN: 9781680507218. $45.95
https://pragprog.com/book/nrclient

Kotlin and Android Development featuring Jetpack

Start building native Android apps the modern way in Kotlin with Jetpack's expansive set of tools, libraries, and best practices. Learn how to create efficient, resilient views with Fragments and share data between the views with ViewModels. Use Room to persist valuable data quickly, and avoid NullPointerExceptions and Java's verbose expressions with Kotlin. You can even handle asynchronous web service calls elegantly with Kotlin coroutines. Achieve all of this and much more while building two full-featured apps, following detailed, step-by-step instructions.

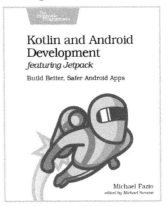

Michael Fazio
(444 pages) ISBN: 9781680508154. $49.95
https://pragprog.com/book/mfjetpack

Learn to Program, Third Edition

It's easier to learn how to program a computer than it has ever been before. Now everyone can learn to write programs for themselves—no previous experience is necessary. Chris Pine takes a thorough, but lighthearted approach that teaches you the fundamentals of computer programming, with a minimum of fuss or bother. Whether you are interested in a new hobby or a new career, this book is your doorway into the world of programming.

Chris Pine
(230 pages) ISBN: 9781680508178. $45.95
https://pragprog.com/book/ltp3

Intuitive Python

Developers power their projects with Python because it emphasizes readability, ease of use, and access to a meticulously maintained set of packages and tools. The language itself continues to improve with every release: writing in Python is full of possibility. But to maintain a successful Python project, you need to know more than just the language. You need tooling and instincts to help you make the most out of what's available to you. Use this book as your guide to help you hone your skills and sculpt a Python project that can stand the test of time.

David Muller
(140 pages) ISBN: 9781680508239. $26.95
https://pragprog.com/book/dmpython

Modern CSS with Tailwind

Tailwind CSS is an exciting new CSS framework that allows you to design your site by composing simple utility classes to create complex effects. With Tailwind, you can style your text, move your items on the page, design complex page layouts, and adapt your design for devices from a phone to a wide-screen monitor. With this book, you'll learn how to use the Tailwind for its flexibility and its consistency, from the smallest detail of your typography to the entire design of your site.

Noel Rappin
(90 pages) ISBN: 9781680508185. $26.95
https://pragprog.com/book/tailwind

Apple Game Frameworks and Technologies

Design and develop sophisticated 2D games that are as much fun to make as they are to play. From particle effects and pathfinding to social integration and monetization, this complete tour of Apple's powerful suite of game technologies covers it all. Familiar with Swift but new to game development? No problem. Start with the basics and then layer in the complexity as you work your way through three exciting—and fully playable—games. In the end, you'll know everything you need to go off and create your own video game masterpiece for any Apple platform.

Tammy Coron
(504 pages) ISBN: 9781680507843. $51.95
https://pragprog.com/book/tcswift

Programming Phoenix 1.4

Don't accept the compromise between fast and beautiful: you can have it all. Phoenix creator Chris McCord, Elixir creator José Valim, and award-winning author Bruce Tate walk you through building an application that's fast and reliable. At every step, you'll learn from the Phoenix creators not just what to do, but why. Packed with insider insights and completely updated for Phoenix 1.4, this definitive guide will be your constant companion in your journey from Phoenix novice to expert as you build the next generation of web applications.

Chris McCord, Bruce Tate and José Valim
(356 pages) ISBN: 9781680502268. $45.95
https://pragprog.com/book/phoenix14

The Pragmatic Bookshelf

The Pragmatic Bookshelf features books written by professional developers for professional developers. The titles continue the well-known Pragmatic Programmer style and continue to garner awards and rave reviews. As development gets more and more difficult, the Pragmatic Programmers will be there with more titles and products to help you stay on top of your game.

Visit Us Online

This Book's Home Page
https://pragprog.com/book/sgdpelixir
Source code from this book, errata, and other resources. Come give us feedback, too!

Keep Up to Date
https://pragprog.com
Join our announcement mailing list (low volume) or follow us on twitter @pragprog for new titles, sales, coupons, hot tips, and more.

New and Noteworthy
https://pragprog.com/news
Check out the latest pragmatic developments, new titles and other offerings.

Save on the ebook

Save on the ebook versions of this title. Owning the paper version of this book entitles you to purchase the electronic versions at a terrific discount.

PDFs are great for carrying around on your laptop—they are hyperlinked, have color, and are fully searchable. Most titles are also available for the iPhone and iPod touch, Amazon Kindle, and other popular e-book readers.

Send a copy of your receipt to support@pragprog.com and we'll provide you with a discount coupon.

Contact Us

Online Orders:	*https://pragprog.com/catalog*
Customer Service:	*support@pragprog.com*
International Rights:	*translations@pragprog.com*
Academic Use:	*academic@pragprog.com*
Write for Us:	*http://write-for-us.pragprog.com*
Or Call:	+1 800-699-7764

Milton Keynes UK
Ingram Content Group UK Ltd.
UKHW050623140624
444011UK00016B/147

9 781680 508192